EXCUSE ME, SIR!

MEMOIR OF A BUTCH

EXCUSE ME, SIR!

MEMOIR OF A BUTCH

SHALEY HOWARD

For my LGBTQ+ family and anyone struggling with addiction—
You are stronger than you think

CONTENTS

INTRODUCTION

I was a 40-year-old out lesbian, who enjoyed a successful business, traveled the world extensively, owned multiple properties, and seemed to thrive. I had all of this despite the obstacle's life had served me from the get-go. I thought I had persevered and overcome those impediments, but in reality, I had learned to simply navigate around them, continually ignoring the multiple elephants in the room. Trying to live the motto, "ignorance is bliss" apparently had consequences.

"Shaley! Oh, for fuck's sake, Shaley, wake up!" I heard in Amy's barely audible voice. Managing to open my eyes slightly, and with blurred vision, I saw her hovering over me, fading in and out of focus. I think she was still talking, or yelling, at me to do something. Then everything went dark.

Now I'm being watched under a microscope, curled in a fetal position in a renovated dorm-room-turned-rehabilitation center. I was horrified as the reality of what my life had become crashed down around me in flames. I laid there trembling, not from withdrawals, but from the fear of the unknown. I was swallowed by a blackhole of loneliness and despair. Everything I thought I was, everything I had, all of it was stripped away.

I'd woken up squinting in pain two days earlier, fully clothed on my grime-covered living room carpet, head pounding and dazed. Wiping the drool off the side of my cheek, I wondered how long I'd been laying there. *What time is it? What day is it?* I tried to sit up, but some invisible force hit my head with lightning white pain, crumpling me to the floor. Laying there trying to recover, my eyes focused on the empty beer bottles under my couch. Those bottles of alcohol had so kindly taken the edge off my withdrawals. But with that temporary relief came the inevitable, pain-driven realization: I had hit rock bottom.

Tears trickled down my face. *What happened to me?* I thought. This was quickly followed with something more urgent. *I need a hit. Or a drink. I feel them. They're coming back.* "'They" were the excruciating pains from opioid withdrawals. The headache I felt from my alcohol-induced hangover was nothing compared to what was coming. Somehow, I managed to get up and find a bottle of alcohol in my barren kitchen cabinets—lucky me. This bottle however was Gin, not beer. *Ugh, really Gin?* I hated Gin. But relief was relief. Pushing past my hesitation, I took a big swig. *Please, please, please let it be enough this time.* I begged.

How does a 40-year-old-lesbian who enjoyed a successful business, traveled the world, and seemed to thrive, end up passed out face down in my own drool? On the TV this is where the screen starts to warp with skewed waves and scaled harp music magically taking us back to Shaley's childhood.

ONE

BUTCH!

Some people think we choose the lives we want to live. They think somehow, in another spiritual dimension, we personally decide what journey we want ride out and experience. If this idea is true, I wonder what the hell I was thinking. Yes please, I'd like to be born female with a more masculine appearance, as a homosexual, in a culture and time period that is full of sexism and, oh yeah—hates gay people. But I'm getting ahead of my own story.

I was an inherently optimistic and jovial kid, laughing a lot and being content most of the time. Around my 5th birthday, everything darkened and became more complicated. I don't actually remember Mom and Dad being married, even though I saw photos of us as a happy family. All I remember was fighting, yelling, and tears. And being scared—a lot.

When they split, Mom, well, disappeared. Not literally, but emotionally and mentally she was often off in la-la land. I believe something broke inside her that she couldn't, or didn't know how, to repair. When she was at home, she didn't seem to notice us much. She was preoccupied and we were just moving objects in the house. Prior to the divorce, she was attentive and engaging, often bursting into our rooms singing the *Carpenters* hit song, "Top of the World" to us, her audience. Then playfully dance, although with Mom it was more like an awkward back-and-forth bobbing, nudging us with her hips. Even with our eyerolls, we'd eventually sing along until our voices turned into belly-aching giggles. But when my dad asked for a divorce, she became distant and distraught. No longer the mother we knew. Instead of *being* her world, we simply occupied it.

I was a latchkey kid, a term in the late 1970's that referred to kids who, in many ways, raised themselves because their parents were absent. Before school, I'd get myself ready and fix my own breakfast, which was usually whatever cereal I found in the cabinets. It was a seriously good morning if Captain Crunchberries was staring down at me. *Why yes! I think I will have some fake berries, Cap'n!* Even if I did walk away with gums bleeding from munching on the artificial jagged little berries—worth it.

Most days no one else was around except my sister Laurie. We were close in age, but she was still a few years older, with an earlier school schedule, leaving before I did. My other sister, who also lived with us at the time, was Cynthia. She was six years older, so from an 8-year old's perspective—ancient. Cynthia seemed almost other-worldly to me at the time, always trying to speak in some alien language only grownups understood. Being the eldest sister, we'd often tease her when she'd start explaining the world to us, in some over-the-top patronizing way, "You *kids* just don't know". Each time we'd laugh and snort, "OK, *Mom*."

Though we teased her relentlessly for pretending she was some old wise woman, ironically it *was* Cynthia I'd turn to occasionally for maternal comfort. Once, I found myself completely turned around and lost at the local mall. My heart increasingly raced as I started making frantic, panicky circles, desperately searching for Laurie's familiar face. Before having a complete meltdown, I did the only thing I could think of; I picked up the payphone and called Cynthia.

She kept me preoccupied with her monotone, Mom-like re-assuring words, asking me to describe the people walking around. "What are they wearing?" she calmly asked. I'd tell her and she'd make funny comments about my descriptions, probably knowing if she kept me distracted and in one place, Laurie would eventual-ly find me. Even in my moment of anxiety, I *still* made fun of her superior-sounding tenor with a snotty, "OK *Mom*," I was a tween and contractually obligated to act like a thankless jerk as stated in the -'*Guidelines for Teen Behavior*'- rulebook, section 214.

No matter what time of day it was, it never mattered to me if anyone was home or not. I was used to taking care of myself. Well, except if lost at the mall. Some mornings, when Mom did happen to get up at the same time as me, she was usually rushing out the door to teach. As a single parent, the weight of everything, now fell on her shoulders. She was a professor at Lewis and Clark College, *and* an elementary school music teacher. Up at dawn and back at dusk. I never understood how she managed both jobs, but I got used to our silent house.

In the afternoon when I'd return home, it was once again just me, our cat Pyewacket, and Dolche our golden retriever. The moment I opened the door, they both clamored for my atten-tion. Pyewacket would nearly trip me with her furry body coiling around my feet, while Dolche would knock me repeatedly, joyous-ly bouncing up and down as if I'd been gone for weeks. He was sweet—not the sharpest tool in the shed, but sweet. "*Dude*," I'd say while laughing each time I attempted to push Dolche away and pick up Pyewacket. She'd immediately start in with her deafening purr, which was only amplified as it echoed throughout the empty house. Then Dolche, Pyewacket and I would begin our afternoon routine of TV and cinnamon toast.

The funny thing was, I was perfectly content. I'd sit and watch *Batman and Robin* or *Gilligan's Island*, with both of them orbiting me, as if I was their sun. Dolche would casually slide next to me while I was eating, then look up with his soft, enormous brown eyes, knowing I was an easy sucker. Eventually I'd playfully sigh, *"Fine,"* and hand him my crust. Meanwhile all Pyewacket wanted was for Dolche to go away so she could purr in peace on my lap. Whatever their individual motives, they were there—always—right by my side.

I don't remember a time I wasn't a major tomboy. I loved anything to do with sports, toy cars, and stuffed animals. My sisters on the other hand, had a ridiculous supply of Barbie dolls, and the houses and cars to match. (Wait, was my Bionic *Six Million Dollar Man* toy a doll?) Theirs of course included Ken. Where would the Barbie world be without a man? A man without any genitals by the way. I discovered this when I took apart my sisters' Barbies and casually distributed the various parts around our house just to fuck with them. The moment I heard the long scream of, "Mom!" I'd smile deviously. *My job here is done.* Mom wasn't going to help. Even when we'd run to her pleading for condemnation and justice, she would casually acknowledge us and in a nonchalant, dismissive manner say, "You girls figure it out". But I digress.

I was often called big boned, which meant I was taller, bigger, and more masculine looking than a lot of girls my age. Being labeled a "big-boned girl" was an acceptable, albeit strange, label at the time. Ultimately, it was used to make *other* people feel comfortable around girls who didn't fit the stereotypical male/female archetypes. Heaven forbid I walk with my hands in my jean pockets. "Shaley, you're so beautiful. Stop acting like a boy with your hands in your pockets. Stand up straight." Not sure why hands in my pockets was boy-like but according to my mom, it was. I'm guessing it made me look aloof and casual. I was told, "Put your legs together," in my mother's overly loud whisper. Was my body language too loose, too casual, too male? I didn't know.

I only knew that each time I'd hear those words, my body would recoil and fill with tension. It was hard enough being so tall as a young girl, always standing out, towering over others, whether I wanted to or not. But at least hunching over I felt less obvious. Until Mom would publicly "recommend" I change my posture, take my hands out of my pockets and act more "ladylike". I would correct my body language and carry on, appearing confident. But inside, I was sure my fragile emotional state would collapse like a house of cards at any moment; always second guessing everything and unsure how to move through the world correctly.

In many ways, I was your typical suburban, painfully awkward kid. Taller than most but especially the boys. I wanted desperately to be seen, and at the same time longed to blend in and never be seen. I know, the essence of a teenager's life. *Look at me! Notice me! Wait, no, don't look at me! Leave me alone!* Unfortunately, even when I tried, there was no escape from sticking out. It wasn't just my height and body language that was a problem. When I say I was a tomboy, yes, I was a little girl who liked more stereotypical "boy" activities. But I also looked like a boy. A boy with long hair. And for the longest time, I could not have cared less what anyone thought. Then, I realized that most girls around me *were* paying attention to their outward appearance. Soon I began to notice the world around me.

Around the age of nine, I realized the once endearing way I'd been misgendered as a young child was no longer charming, and definitely not acceptable. Now when strangers thought they were complimenting my mom with, "Oh what a cute little boy you have," it only seemed to irritate, and I'm guessing embarrass her too. Surprisingly when this happened, she never admonished me, but the unaware stranger definitely received a swift and abrupt correction of my true gender. I guess she was the only one allowed to "correct" me. Wearing dirt covered T-shirts, mismatching socks and sporting a disheveled haircut was commonplace. Even with four sisters who lived for hair, makeup, and fashion, it took me years to even think about my outward appearance.

My aunt and uncle would drive from Idaho to visit during our summers. Each time they'd come, I'd fidget back and forth tingling with anticipation in our driveway for their station wagon to round the corner. Then I'd wave enthusiastically with both arms in the air, as if guiding in a jumbo jet. The sound of my aunt's overly loud *swish, swish* polyester skirt rubbing against her thick pantyhose always reached me long before she actually did. Then, in an unspoken cue, she'd lovingly smile down with her thin lips and make a polite yet obligatory kiss on my cheek. I'd respond with my own polite yet obligatory, "Hi, Aunt Ethel," as she sauntered past.

My uncle would then step up, plop his suitcase down, and with a planet-sized grin exclaim, "Who wants candy?!" This was met with screams of, "Me! Me! Me!" as we all jumped up and down, eagerly awaiting our sweet surprise. He'd fill our open hands and wink, as if sharing some sort of club secret. We knew what his wink meant. In addition to being a genuine present, it was also a bribe. We couldn't stand our aunts' overpowering rose perfume that permeated everything and lingered long after they left; and he knew it. My aunt, however, loved it and never went anywhere without it. Candy treats helped quiet our sophomoric commentary during their stays.

The summer I turned 10, and after everyone was settled, my aunt and Mom immediately gravitated to our living room sofa, eager to catch up. They'd chatter nonstop, seemingly unaware of my presence on the floor in front of them. I giggled to myself as their steady stream of words filled the room. They reminded me of the overly talkative, gossipy Blue Jays outside my window every morning. As they continued their banter, I sat quietly preoccupied on our rug, perfectly content, spinning my favorite Mack toy truck in circles with accompanying, *RRoooom! Rrrrooom!* sounds. Dolche sat at my side watching, thrilled by—well, anything I was doing.

"She'll grow out of it," Aunt Ethel confidently told my mother, as if I wasn't in the room. My back stiffened. I supposed this was an attempt from my aunt to comfort my poor mother suffering a boy-like daughter. My stomach twisted in knots as her heavy words sank in. The lightness that had filled me moments before was now heavy and weighted, like a wilting balloon, hovering an inch above the floor.

Pretending to be bored with my truck, I casually slid it over and wrapped my arms around Dolche, burying my face in his golden fur, deciding to play with him instead. I was hoping this would appease them, and they'd go back to their babbling. I didn't exactly understand why, but something told me I needed to stop playing with my truck. At least in front of them.

Like a distress signal from a flare gun, another message had been received. Reminding, while also warning me, of the inescapable male/female roles I needed to follow. Being mistaken for a boy by then, was embarrassing for everyone involved, including me. As I developed and matured, it was obvious something about my appearance made people uncomfortable. Standing in front of the mirror that afternoon, carefully studying my reflection, a mixture of resentment and confusion churned inside. "What's wrong with my body?" I thought, as I fought angry tears. The shape of my body was *slightly* different than a few girls my age perhaps. Mine was more like a capital I, then S—not many curves happening. But most of my friends looked similar to me, almost androgynous, simply because of our age.

As I considered this, memories of all the negative comments I'd overheard from strangers, and even my own family, flashed through my mind. I began to understand. Being mistaken for a boy wasn't simply because of my body. It was about my outward appearance *and* behavior. And since the shape of my body clearly wasn't going to cooperate, I had to change the way I dressed and start behaving more like a girl. Funnily enough, until everyone started commenting, I had never realized how problematic and threatening my outward image and "tomboy" behavior had been.

This was a time when there were very clear social distinctions between male and female genders. Toy aisles for boys were blue, and girls were pink. Boys had toy truck and cars in their aisle, and girls had dolls. There were not a lot of positive, constructive conversations about gender identity and sexual orientation happening. At least not in my world. Yet on top of my "rough" boyish appearance and disorderly "unladylike" behavior, I had a far bigger problem. I was also gay. And I mean *Gay* with a capital G. Welcome to my living nightmare of puberty.

I remember my first teacher crush in grade school. Her name Mrs. Aguirre and she was so beautiful. I found myself, every morning, discreetly checking that all my clothes matched, my buttons were buttoned correctly, and my hair was perfect. Well, as perfect as a Mary Lou Retton tomboy bob could be. The problem was that whenever she called on me, I froze. My heart pounded so loud I was sure all my classmates could hear it. Most of the time I could barely remember my name, let alone the answer to whatever she was asking. I was completely unable to make eye contact; certain she would see through my façade right into my desperate love for her.

My parents probably thought I had a learning disability, watching my grades plummet that year. And Mrs. Aguirre probably thought I hated her when all I longed for was her undivided attention. She never saw inside my Pee-Chee notebook, covered with A + S heart doodles. When some of the girls in my class accidentally saw them, however, they taunted me, "Ooooh…Shaley likes Mrs. Aguirre! That's *so* gay!" I promptly replied, "You guys are so stupid. The "'A'" isn't Mrs. Aguirre. And I'm *so* not gay. Gross." Then I quickly put away my Pee-Chee.

It was better to hide and immediately defend yourself from these sorts of accusations. I'd seen how often Bobby, an effeminate looking boy in our school, was constantly harassed in the hallways, often being ridiculed mercilessly. "Hey faggot!" Steve, a notoriously known troublemaker, said one afternoon standing with a group of friends by his locker. Bobby kept walking, head hung low, not daring to make eye contact. They all laughed as he passed, adding, "hey sissy boy, stop checking me out." No one came to Bobby's defense.

The worst was when I would hear adults describing someone who was, you know, "that way". That *way* was gay, and it was always said as a whisper in the middle of a sentence as something to be pitied. "Poor thing, what a shame." As though whoever they were referring to intentionally chose to be gay and lead *that* lifestyle, so all hope was lost. Each time a conversation went in that direction, I'd sink into my body, attempting to remain incognito, praying no eyes would glance my way.

One sunny September afternoon in 7th grade, I was walking home from school with my friends. Well, actually they were about a block ahead of me. I'd fallen back from the group, lost in thought, gazing up at the brilliant fall colors spreading across the Maple trees that lined our street. The familiar sounds of lawn mowers, dogs barking, and kids playing filled the air. My neighbors and I, many of whom were also my classmates and friends, would hang out regularly playing tag, hide 'n' seek, or whatever game we created. Usually until the streetlight came on. It had always felt safe.

Suddenly I was jerked out of my daydream when someone yelled, "Butch!" Confused, I looked over to see the fleeting faces of three young men laughing, hanging out the windows of their truck as they disappeared in a cloud of dust. Since I was walking alone, it was obvious who the insult was targeting—me.

Everyone in front of me immediately turned. Momentarily my world went dark, and I heard the *clunk* of a spotlight being turned on, aimed directly at me. My jaw clenched as a mixture of inexplicable anger and fear surged through my body, and my eyes pricked with tears. Even though it was warm outside, I pulled my hoodie up over my head trying to appear oblivious, hoping to go unnoticed. I desperately begged that my out-of-place, offensive boyish, now "butch" body would disappear. Or, somehow miraculously blend into my suburbanite background—as if *it* and *I* belonged. If I had been any closer to the group, they surely would have noticed my face, flushed with embarrassment and self-loathing.

I looked up and pretended to dramatically search my surroundings, trying to play dumb. I shrugged my shoulders and laughed, as if to say, "Who were those guys yelling at?" then turned away to hide my mortification. *Do not cry in front of them, Shaley. Don't you fucking cry.* I wanted nothing more in that moment than to join in their gawking and aloof giddiness. To be part of their laughter while looking around for some butch-looking, mannish freak. I longed to blend in and not be singled out—to imagine the fly-by insult was meant for someone else. But it was clear who it was meant for, and it certainly wouldn't be the last time I was targeted.

TWO
WHAT HAPPENED TO MOM?

I t was confusing to us how much our neighbor's loved Mom. Not because she wasn't a generous and likeable person. We just happened to experience a different woman than the one she showed the outside world, especially after the divorce. I still don't know the exact reason for my parents' divorce. I mean, shit, I was five, how the hell would I know? Perhaps it was finances or a midlife crisis. Perhaps my dad fell out of love and had an affair. Or perhaps, like so many others, the relationship ran its course and it was time to let go. My guess is it was a combination of a lot of things just waiting to implode.

I was aware, even at a young age, that most people wear a slightly different, let's just say, more "'improved'" persona in public. No one wants to reveal their ugly side, or possibly *sides*, to acquaintances or strangers. But it was surprising to us that no one else saw what we did. The other side of her—the break downs, the mood swings, the person who frequently wasn't present even when in our presence.

Over time her temperament, at least in front of us, became more erratic. Her moods weren't severe, but enough that I unconsciously wore a low-level nervous vibration. Always slightly on edge, trying to anticipate what might happen next. Whenever she was home and especially if she entered my room as a teenager, I'd hold my breath feeling my body tense. I never knew who would greet me. Would it be unaware, preoccupied Mom? Or irritated, unpredictable Mom? Or kind, upbeat Mom?

I'd instinctively find myself slightly bracing for impact anytime I heard the sound of our car pulling onto our gravel driveway. Would it be a good or bad day? Perhaps when I was much younger, before their divorce, her melodramatic, uncontrolled mood swings were trivial and went unnoticed. But afterwards, her emotional state magnified significantly. Like an inherently joyful, emotionally stable person that drinks too much alcohol, then becomes the ridiculously entertaining, happy drunk. The same can be said with a resentful, unhappy person. Alcohol intensifies their core state of being and often turns them into the uncontrollable, angry drunk.

With Mom, it seemed like the divorce was the catalyst that only amplified her propensity towards emotional instability. If a grimacing, stone-face Mom walked in the door, my pulse would start to rise with strange, confusing apprehension. I longed for the mom I vaguely remembered when I was a small child. The person that frequently wore a warm smile that would, and still occasionally could—radiate trust, affection, and enduring love. The outside world got to see her overly-kind, generous, attentive side regularly. But for me and my sisters, over time it became crapshoot as to who would show up.

My parents divorced after 20 years of marriage. I've always believed that what truly screws up our adult lives is our inability to maintain healthy relationships. Teaching kids how to understand or manage emotions was never part of any classroom curriculum. We certainly were not taught how to overcome, or even see, the mounting baggage left from childhood trauma. We worked on our intellectual growth, while our emotional and psychological growth received little or no guidance. So, it's no big surprise that later, when an intimate relationship comes along, we're knocked on our asses. A tidal wave of inexperience and emotional ignorance hits us like a tsunami.

Growing up in an era where no one talked about dysfunctional families or divorce, my mother was—in many ways—a victim of the time. Our family had the outward appearance everyone wanted. A big four-bedroom house in the suburbs, a safe neighborhood where kids could stay out past dark, good schools and our trusty olive green, wood paneled family station wagon. Yeah, we were *styling*. On the surface, it was nice. I always had food, clothing, and shelter. I always felt physically safe and had plenty of friends. But if you were to look closer, the cracks were obvious.

Mom was constantly absent either teaching her classes or finishing her PhD. She was no stranger to hard work. And with a house full of daughters and a mortgage, working hard was a necessity. She was also a member of Mensa, so clearly intellectually mature. I mean, the woman was an extraordinary conversationalist and could discuss any topic under the sun without falter, in great detail. I would later learn, however, that being intellectually mature doesn't necessarily correlate to emotional maturity. Still, she was loved by many.

On her 50th birthday our house seemed to be bursting at its wooden seams with friends celebrating her life. Just squeezing through the wall of people took a solid ten minutes. "Can you believe this crowd?" I told Laurie with a mouth full of birthday cake. "Yeah, it's unreal. I never knew she had so many friends." But really, why would we? Growing up we were, well, *kids*. And kids by nature are usually self-absorbed with their own friends and drama. Plus, Mom never had friends over. We'd hear her talk occasionally about random people but never thought much of it. Also, it is highly probable she had mentioned her friends and we never paid attention having "we only care about our own lives" selective hearing.

"Your mother is a wonderful woman, you know," I heard in a soft, shaky voice at my side. Preoccupied with my plate of cake, I looked up to see Mrs. Jones, who'd lived on our street for over forty years, even after her husband passed away. I hadn't seen her for so long I almost didn't recognize her. Staring down at her, I thought, "Either I grew into Sasquatch or she shrank into an adorable, wrinkled turtle." Realizing I was being rude and weirdly awkward, I tried to compose myself while wiping frosting from my chin. "Mrs. Jones!" I enthusiastically coughed out while trying to swallow my remaining cake. I bent over to give her a gentle hug, thinking I might crush her with my mammoth body. "It's so nice to see you!" I said and proceeded to make "'how have you been?'" small talk.

In many ways, the neighborhood I grew up in was an idyllic place to raise a family. The loudest sounds you'd ever hear were kids yelling, dogs barking, or bouncing balls. Maybe the occasional radio music from a passing car. Everyone knew everyone. Whenever she was around, Mom would stop and chat with our neighbors, but especially Mrs. Jones. I think she worried about her after her husband died. Even after working long days, Mom would often still make a point to check in on her. Mrs. Jones always seemed perfectly content to me in her garden humming or gazing out her front window at the drizzling rain so common in Oregon. Yet her face did seem to beam with delight when she noticed Mom coming up her walkway.

After returning from the grocery store, Mom would occasionally ask, "Shaley, run these over to Mrs. Jones, honey. She'll really appreciate them." "'Them'" was usually some little treat like a box of cookies. And my response was generally, "You know who else would appreciate these Mom?" Seriously, there was no way Mrs. Jones was gonna eat all of them. Why couldn't we have them?

And by *we* I meant *me*. But each time I made the delivery, without pause, Mrs. Jones would light up and gush with appreciation, which in turn made *me* beam with delight.

There were five of us growing up, including me; all girls. Beth, my stepsister, and my older sister, Cynthia, who we called "Mom" when she tried to mom us. I was the baby of the bunch until my half-sister Larisa came along. This meant that I could get away with all sorts of asshole, annoying behavior, initiated 100% of the time by me. If Mom did ever get involved, it was usually to tell my older sisters to *Stop*. The younger one (me) rarely got blamed. Yet despite our occasional quarrels bound to happen with so many siblings, my sisters were also my friends, especially Laurie. We were closest in age and endured much of our dysfunctional family drama at the same time so inevitably, became each other's lifeline.

My sister Laurie loved Shaun Cassidy. Her walls were covered with *Teen Beat* posters of him smiling with his pearly white teeth, doe eyes, and long feathered hair. Whenever she wanted company, she'd try to lure me in saying, "Shaun Cassidy is everywhere," which is super creepy if you're a lesbian who's not at all interested in boys. Also, just super creepy. Wanting to maintain the illusion of being straight, I always grinned and pretended to eagerly long to be under the gaze of the teen heartthrob. "Well, OK, since you put it that way. Who doesn't want to look up at him all night?!" I'm fairly certain if I had suggested she sleep in my room instead, with posters of Billie Jean King staring down on us, it may have prompted a very different response. But either way it didn't matter. Even if it meant pretending to like Shaun Cassidy, I loved hanging out with Laurie.

One evening, Mom called Laurie and me out to the living room. She was sitting next to this slightly overweight man, who had on a polyester suit and a fat matching striped tie. I kept staring up at him, wondering if he was OK. I could see the skin of his neck bulging over his white collar, his face was bright red. It looked like his tie was too tight and he might be suffocating. My fascination with his appearance quickly vanished though when Mom announced, "Girls, this is your *new* dad." Confused, I said matter-of-factly, "He's not my dad. My dad lives in an apartment. We've been there."

Seriously, what adult brings a stranger into a house then expects another man's children to welcome him with open arms? You can't just add and subtract a mom or dad from a child's life simply because you fucked up your adult relationship. And poor Larry, our apparent "new dad". I often wonder if he felt shell-shocked when she said that to us. It would definitely explain his crimson face. It's a lot of pressure to take on a brand-new family made up of all girls. Needless to say, he was not going to be our "new dad" and we pretty much hated him from the start.

Despite remarrying, for my mother, letting go after the divorce didn't seem to be an option. Something had broken her psyche. Maybe if she had been in her right mind, she would have never used us as pawns against our dad, or "Chuck". When they split up, his name was no longer "Dad", it became, "that *Chuck*". And she would spit it out with such noticeable venom, we couldn't help but giggle. We were, however, smart enough to never to use the word "Dad". (In front of her, at least.) This kind, overly generous, wildly intelligent woman seemed to lose sight of anything of true importance. At least, that's what I tell myself. It's still hard to accept that your own mother would choose anything over her own kids.

The battle for custody and the house was never-ending. Like I said, I wasn't sure what exactly my dad did, but all my mom seemed to do was cry. She would sob in her room for hours, sometimes all day, completely checked out. I would sit outside her bedroom door on the carpet and listen. I wasn't sure what I was supposed to do. Sometimes I would softly creep into her bedroom, up to the side of her bed and ask, "Are you OK, Mom?" But the agonizing crying—wailing—didn't stop. Sometimes she would curl up in a ball and make such deep, guttural sounds that it seemed like she was writhing from physical pain. I wondered if maybe she *had* injured herself physically. I knew my friend Suzy had yelled and screamed like that when she fell the previous summer. Maybe something had happened to my mom that I couldn't see. I would try soothing her, wrapping my skinny little arms as far around her as possible, hoping to help. Sometimes she would acknowledge me there at her side, but mostly I felt invisible and useless. I'd eventually tire and go back to my bedroom or outside to play.

Once, I was reminding Laurie casually that, "Dad's coming to pick us up at 5:00," not realizing my mom was in the room. Her instant sideways glare chilled me, and I immediately regretted my choice of words. The worst part about the divorce wasn't Mom being absent so much, it was that she forgot we needed her unconditional love. We were her children; we were supposed to come first. At the bare minimum, we shouldn't have been used as pawns against our dad for revenge. We became collateral.

After my dad moved out, we were only allowed to see him on our "visitation days" as Mom put it. Laurie and I would sit in front of our big picture window in the kitchen, excitedly waiting for him to pull up. Then we'd yell to Mom, "He's here! Love you!" making sure not to use the 'D' word. After getting the usual silent response, we'd quietly close the front door and pile into Dad's little blue Datsun. It was a sort of adventure for us, like a mini vacation.

Even though Dad's apartment was small, it was cozy and had a few pieces of recognizable furniture, like our favorite brown threadbare sofa with its squishy cushions. Familiarity made our visits more comfortable, but ultimately what truly made us feel at ease was being wanted. Dad always seemed interested in whatever we shared, even our long, never-ending stories. He listened, laughed, and made us feel important.

One time while visiting, we were watching the *Brady Bunch*, you know, the show with the perfect all-American family, and Dad said he had to run to the store. He assured us he'd be right back and locked the door as he left. We had each other, so we weren't fazed at all by being left alone. The fact was, we were used to it with Mom. Like I said, even when she was home, she often wasn't present. Half the time I don't think she even knew if *we* were home or not.

Laurie and I had learned to rely on each other for company and comfort. And after Mom and Dad separated, I found myself clinging to her for that comfort a lot. Everything had changed so quickly. Mom seemed to suddenly hate our dad. Phone calls between them were loud and always ended abruptly. And now he had a new apartment he called home, but we still lived with Mom. It was all confusing and scary. Dad tried reassuring us by saying this was just temporary and everything would work out, even though I wasn't sure what that meant. But I adored and trusted him, so as long as he was still around, I figured it would all be OK.

As soon as the door shut, Laurie and I grabbed the chips off the top of the fridge and proceeded to rip open the bag on the shag carpet in front of the TV. Dad couldn't have been gone for more than five minutes when we heard a soft knock on the door. We both froze, me with half-eaten chips hanging from my mouth, and looked at each other. I got up to answer and said timidly, "Who is it?" A restrained voice outside said, "Honey, it's me. Open up." Lacking confidence and thoroughly confused, I looked back at Laurie and whispered, "What do I do?" We both knew there were new rules now. Mom wasn't supposed to be here at Dad's and vice versa. My sister sat there perfectly still, eyes wide, shaking her head slightly in confusion, yet knowing we had to open the door. I mean, she was our mom.

This was a new fear and something we hadn't experienced. It wasn't getting scolded for stealing cookies or being too loud past our bedtime. This was different and we didn't fully understand the game. Our mom was outside asking to come inside. Turning back to a now more insistent knock coming through the door, a new, tough voice inside me thought, "This is stupid. Just go open the door, dummy. It's Mom." Pretending all was normal and pushing past my fear, I hesitantly obeyed, reached up and turned the deadbolt.

Appearing panicky and disheveled with wisps of hairs sticking out, she barely acknowledged me as she pushed the door open and rushed inside. Her Estée Lauder fragrance lingered in the entryway as she ran into the back bedroom, leaving me standing there alone. The cool outside air hit me as I closed the door and quickly walked back over to Laurie. I sat down cross-legged beside her, knees touching, and grasping for her hand. All we heard was the rummaging and clinking sounds of drawers opening and closing. We sat quiet and still, our bodies stiff with tension. We looked back and forth at each other, silently, not knowing what to do. Laurie leaned over, squeezed my hand and whispered, "It's OK." The sound of our mom trespassing carelessly through Dad's belongings blended with the distant dialogue of Mike and Carol Brady, the fictitious loving and attentive parents. The undeniable juxtaposition of our new reality colliding with TV Land's perfect family was palpable.

Minutes—that seemed like hours—passed as Mom frantically rushed back into the living room clutching a manila folder. Her composure instantly changed to surprise, as if remembering we were still there. Like *we* were the intruders. She went from a self-absorbed temperament to one of recognition and apparent concern. Her eyes softened and became more focused. Shifting her weight to one side in order to hide the manila folder behind her back, she stiffened and stared down at us with what we called her "teacher" face. Her jaw clenched and her eyes narrowed. Similar to when you misbehave in school and your teacher's eyes target in on you, and with lips barely moving they say, "Shaley, come up here right now." Perhaps realizing her children were there, confused, and scared, (and let's face it, possible witnesses to her crime), she said in a stern but reassuring tone, "Girls I was never here. No matter what, do not say anything to Chuck, your dad. I'll see you at home. I love you."

Hearts thumping with fear, we both nodded in unison. And then, as quickly as she'd entered, she disappeared. The door shut, leaving us alone in heavy stunned silence with only the sound of the TV playing in the background. The lightning speed at which we went from giddy, carefree children to confronting the confusing weightiness of adulthood was astonishing. We sat there holding hands, not knowing what had happened or what to do. We had no words to describe it nor the understanding necessary. We sat quietly, completely numb. Finally, I broke the silence, "What are we gonna do? I mean, Dad will be back soon. Do we tell him?" Laurie shook her head. Repeatedly, she shook her head while looking at me with glistening eyes. We were both dangerously close to opening a floodgate of tears.

The next thing we heard were the startling sounds of keys jangling outside the door. The same door that my mom had just darted out of. It was Dad. Would he know? Would he smell her perfume still hanging in the air? An enormous sense of relief fused with anxiety filled me. "Dad's back!" I blurted to Laurie, maybe needing to reassure myself it was going to be OK. But was it? He cracked open the door, juggling a couple brown grocery bags in one hand while struggling to remove the key in the other.

Even before setting the groceries down, he knew something was wrong. With blank faces, our eyes welling up with tears were a dead giveaway. "What happened? What's wrong?" he said. I was trying hard not to panic but could feel small tremors taking over. "Mom," I said quietly, "She came by. We didn't know what to do so we opened the door." His face instantly changed from parental concern to anger.

In the seconds it took for him to walk to the kitchen and put down the bags, my little body was ambushed by a flurry of emotions. Was he going to be mad at us too? The immediate feeling of betrayal towards my mom was already overwhelming as I tried to hold back tears, now stinging my heated cheeks. She told me not to say anything and the first thing I did was tell on her. Even with my father reassuring my sister and me that we did nothing wrong, I felt besieged with confusion and fear.

"What did she do? Did she take anything?" he urgently asked. Underneath those seemingly simple and benign words was a palpable undercurrent of emotional desperation and anger even a child could feel. Laurie and I shook our heads because, really, we didn't know what she stole. We didn't even know if stealing was what she did. My dad gave us a long hug then retreated to the back room.

Once again, we sat there alone. The TV had been switched off. The only sounds we heard came from the creaking of tenants upstairs, the low rumbling of distant traffic, and my dad rummaging through his things. We moved closer together on the cushions and held hands. Suddenly we heard, "God dammit, Sylvia!" and then bits of a muffled one-sided conversation. "You're too much…." and "I'll see you in court!" Then there was a clang and the echoing ring of the phone being slammed onto the receiver.

He came back and reassured us again that everything was OK, and we weren't in trouble. Walking into the kitchen he casually asked us if we were hungry. I immediately jumped up, yelling, "Yes!" desperately wanting the drama to end. Laughing at my eager response, he picked me up and plopped me down on a vinyl dining chair. Laurie came and sat down while he proceeded to unpack the groceries and prepare dinner. Mom wasn't mentioned at all.

We both dreaded going back home, unsure if Mom would be angry at us for our betrayal or if nothing would be said at all.

I had gleefully floated through the illusion of a safe and limitless world, but that had changed. It now came with rules and boundaries attached to my parents. I needed to be more cautious in what I shared. Some things were safe, and some were best to remain a secret.

THREE

CHRISTMAS SO SOON?

"Santa's coming!" yelled some kid as I walked to class. My stomach immediately clenched. Christmas: that thrilling time of year when so many children were beside themselves with the excitement of the upcoming holiday. For us, it was a mixed bag of emotions. On one hand, Christmas was fantastic, because after the divorce we ended up with two Christmases. Twice as many presents, two Christmas trees, two Santa visits, two stockings to open—you get the picture. On the other hand, usually just after Thanksgiving, Mom and Dad would begin fighting over where the "girls" should spend Christmas Eve.

Laurie, Cynthia, and I found ourselves in the middle of *their* never-ending holiday war. "You do want to be here on Christmas girls, *don't you?*" Mom would ask, not making much of an effort to hide the obvious guilt trip embedded in the question. We'd give her our obligatory nod of agreement while looking down, trying to appear as non-committal as possible while also wearing our 'go team mom' faces. Then there was Dad, who never openly pressured us, but when the subject of Christmas did come up, the room would immediately fill with a silent, foreboding tension. Trying to please both parents was like having a fear of heights while walking a tightrope 60 feet up and no safety net below. We knew no matter how hard we tried, inevitably we would fall.

The Christmas visitation schedule had zero flexibility. The courts had decided we would spend Christmas Eve and morning with Mom, then Dad could pick us up on Christmas afternoon. Each year was the same routine. Christmas morning would come with absolute chaos as we tore through our stockings and presents, squealing with delight, leaving nothing but crumpled bits of wrapping paper, mangled bows, and empty boxes scattered everywhere. Then like toddlers eating too much cake, we'd go from manic, frenzied energy to a kind of insulin slump, wanting nothing more than a nap. We'd then remember our second Christmas at Dad's and miraculously we'd be filled with a newfound energy.

Unfortunately, this feeling of enthusiasm was always accompanied by fear. We knew that the moment we finished Christmas with Mom and started carting presents to our room, her mood would shift. Everything we'd just experienced, the laughter and joy of time spent with her, would soon be soured because of Chuck. Dad was never welcome inside my mom's house. He would wait for us in his car as we frantically packed our bags and ran out the door yelling, "Bye, Mom! We love you!" Which was always met with a palpable chilling and silent resentment from my mom. Her intense hatred of my dad, knowing we were going over to be with him, made everyone anxious and threatened to ruin Christmas every year.

Not surprisingly, when my father pushed to change the structure of visitations, our mother firmly said no. I am positive my dad was hurt and desperately wanted us for the holiday, but to his credit he never once demeaned our mom. At least not in front of us. Mom, on the other hand, had no filter. She would call Dad all sorts of names in front of us and mumble her insults loud enough that there was no way to avoid hearing. "That Chuck and his whore." (Referring to my stepmom, who had been married to my dad for at least five years.) "He thinks he can have whatever he wants. Christmas is *my* time." Mom didn't ask us what we wanted; if she had, we wouldn't have been upfront with our answers anyway. If she ever did bring it up, it was manipulative and rhetorical. "You girls don't actually *want* to go over there for Christmas Eve, do you?" The correct response was always an absolute, "No."

We played along out of the sheer fear of crossing her. I don't think we actually knew what the consequences would've been if we opposed her, but her emotional state around my dad was obviously unstable. It had become a weird game of "whack-a-mole" with Mom. Always on guard, never knowing when she'd pop up and be angry with us or completely normal. We didn't fear being grounded or having TV privileges taken away; our punishment was bigger and unknown, which made it even more threatening. I'd learn much later in life that the day-to-day experience of living with someone unstable would cause far more emotional and psychological damage to me, than suffering a few major catastrophes. Should've started saving for counseling then.

We never said anything negative about our father, but we also lacked the courage to defend him. Everything was "Chuck's fault." Years after the divorce—everything—and I mean *everything*. Once, the toilet broke and it was "Chuck's fault!" something went unpaid? "Chuck's fault!" If he had "done this" or "took care of that" none of this would be happening. Everything was "Chuck's fault".

My dad had already started taking action in regard to our Christmas visitations. Because my mother clearly wasn't going to discuss options and cooperate, he was forced to turn to the courts. Unfortunately, this involved us. Why, you may ask, would the courts bring in such young children to testify? I have no idea. You could blame it on it being the late 1970's, though I can't begin to understand any time period when this would be acceptable. But it was. And it happened.

I remember my mother calmly sitting us down, saying, "Girls, we are going to go talk with a nice judge. It's all OK. The judge just wants to ask your opinion regarding where you would like to spend Christmas. OK?" To which I thought, *Um, no, no it wasn't OK! What the hell?* Yes—I swore, even as a kid. As someone who loved both my parents, I thought the answer was obvious. Why not just rotate each year? One year at Dad's for Christmas Eve, the following at Mom's? A ten-year-old could figure out what was equal and fair, even if the adults seemed to lack the same clarity.

The day arrived and my stomach was gurgling, tied up in knots, and my legs felt like they were going to buckle with every step I took. It was similar to how my body reacted to the first day of school every year. People always patted me on the head patronizingly, telling me, "Oh, poor thing. It's just butterflies in your stomach." But my 'butterflies' were always more like angry hornets swarming inside me, fighting to get out. And getting 'out' usually meant something was definitely exiting a certain end of my body. I'd frequently felt so paralyzingly sick when this happened, I'd miss the first day of school.

It was just my sister Laurie and me that morning. I'm not sure why Cynthia wasn't included in the fun. My guess is because she was six years older and wanted nothing to do with Mom's vindictive behavior or the divorce, so got a free pass. My fancy dress shoes Mom made me wear were hand-me downs, and slightly too big, so made loud, echoing clippity-clop sounds. I started pretended to be a horse as we approached the towering courthouse entrance, aloof in my own world, making galloping sounds. Clearly doing anything to escape my reality. But Laurie, knowing me so well and seeing my attempt at disguising my stress by dragging my feet, literally, held my hand tighter while I struggled to gracefully climb the courthouse's marble steps—reassuring me I wasn't alone.

Up until that point in my young life, my knowledge of judges and courts was limited. I thought we'd be greeted by some Perry Mason-like attorney. There would be a jury staring—possibly glaring—at me while I broke down on the stand. I imagined myself yelling, then crying uncontrollably, then confessing as the bailiff appeared to escort me to the big house.

Instead, Laurie and I were ushered into a formal office with dark brown wooden panels and told to wait. We sat there, trying to act like adults while our feet dangled down from the oversized, plush leather chairs. After a few minutes, Laurie asked the receptionist if we could go to the bathroom. I sat there in a daze until I noticed Laurie's eyes glued to me, informing me we were both going—together. I jumped down from the chair and followed-obediently.

Entering the bathroom, I dramatically gagged at the overwhelming smell of industrial bleach that permeated the room. "Ugh, my nose hairs are burning!" I whined, trying to make both of us laugh with my sophomoric behavior. Laurie ignored me and carefully checked under each stall. Then she blurted, "What are we going to do?!" Admittedly, we were both fairly scared and definitely intimidated by that point. We didn't understand why the decision came down to us. We were kids. The pressure was too much. "I don't know," I nervously replied, "What do you think we should do? And where did Mom go?" Laurie, pacing the room, said matter-of-factly, "I don't think she can be in the attorney's office."

I decided to try to pee. Sitting in the stall, plugging my nose from the overly sanitized toilets, I squeaked out a nasally thought, "Maybe we could just say what we think is fair—like switching back and forth each Christmas?" There was no response, just the soft sound of Laurie's shoes on the marble floor. Finishing up, I opened the bathroom stall door and looked at her. We both stopped, momentarily frozen in time, recognizing and sharing the weight and profound hopelessness of our situation. We were back on that tightrope, 60 feet up with no safety net below, knowing no matter how hard we tried, inevitably we would fall.

My sister and I, in some ways, could not have been more different. She was always the responsible sister, the one who respected authority. I did not share that same enthusiasm. I was the bull in the china shop; I had an often-oblivious inability, or perhaps a lack of willingness, to simply follow instructions. I was that kid that incessantly asked, "But why? *Why* can't I do that?" stubbornly pushing until I was grounded or sent to the principal's office.

Up to that point in my life, the usual response I received was, "No. You cannot do that," so I quickly learned it was better to ask forgiveness than permission. I will never understand why anyone in a position of authority would avoid explaining the purpose of a rule. It really would've saved all of us so much time. If there had been logical explanations, I would have minded them. I think. Maybe.

If we were told not to ride double on a bike, then I would be the one convincing Laurie to go against our mother's expressed wishes, telling her, "Just sit behind me. No one needs to know." Because, for me, the lure of the bike ride completely outweighed my mother's admonishments. For Laurie, the accommodating middle child, she'd willingly go along to get along. Then hop on the back, even with me screwing around so much, thinking I was funny, careening and bobbing down an asphalt hill, nearly getting us killed when we inevitably crashed.

I ended up unconscious in the street, then hospitalized with a nasty concussion, while my poor sister had to be helped with even the simplest actions until her busted collarbone healed. My mother, predictably, blew a fuse and part of my "punishment" was to help Laurie dress each morning. Since she couldn't move her arm, someone had to help her. I, of course, did feel bad, but not for breaking a rule. My only guilt was hurting Laurie.

She was the stereotypical pretty girl-next-door, with big doe-like brown eyes, long flowing hair, and a warm inviting smile. She was popular and loved by everyone, especially teachers. On the first day of school, my new teachers would discover I was Laurie's younger sister. Initially, they would beam with delight, and drone on about how wonderful she was and how thrilled they were to have me in their classroom that year. They assumed, of course, that being siblings meant I would be a similar, model student. Usually, it took less than a week for them to change their tune. I would watch their beaming smiles morph into furrowed brows and permanent scowls.

Yet despite our different perspectives on life (and authority), Laurie and I were tight. Even when we'd end up screaming at each other on the tennis court, John McEnroe style, because she did not see that the ball was *clearly* inside the line, we still laughed and had fun. We knew that at the end of the day, we were each other's lifeline in our tumultuous home-life. She was my confidant and touchstone.

As we made our way back to the attorney's office, my body flushed with nervous energy, and everything tensed up. I could feel my dress shirt clinging to my skin and suddenly wished I had done more in the bathroom, as flashbacks of my first day of school "toilet" adventures hit me. Or rather hit my gut. As soon as we entered his office, a tall, lanky attorney greeted us with his shiny, big tooth smile. He stood imposingly behind his enormous desk with a wall of plaques and certificates framing him. Waving us over, he motioned for us to sit onto yet more oversized plush chairs across from him. Once on the chairs, we both kept sinking down so had to continually perform an awkward balancing act just to sit up high enough to see his entire face.

It was all so confusing. From our view, the solution of switching back and forth each year seemed quite logical. They were our parents and we loved them equally. The idea that love could be divided or categorized in different levels of importance hadn't fully been absorbed as part of our language yet. But there we were, being asked to choose one or the other. There was no way out and no way to please both parents. And even though we were unsure what the consequences would be, we knew for certain there would be consequences either way.

I was filled with apprehension, but a small quiet sigh of relief escaped when I saw that Mom was not present. I think they thought that would somehow make it easier on us, or perhaps they'd get a more truthful answer if she wasn't there. "Hello, girls, I'm Steve," he said in a soft, warm tenor. Apparently, Steve just wanted to ask us one simple question. "Where would you like to spend Christmas Eve each year?" Didn't he know that there was no right answer to that question? Did he care? He wouldn't be around for the aftermath.

Laurie shyly said, "I don't care," her "response," a complete lack of response. She did care, of course, but I understood her fear. Laurie was only three years older than me, and yet she was supposed to navigate this grownup world with ease and mastery, all while protecting me. She was my older sister, yes, but neither of us were prepared for this forced adulthood. Not to mention she was never a bold kid. She was the middle child, hated conflict, and always wanted everyone to get along. I loved her for that.

I, on the other hand, was the baby of the bunch—the youngest child, ready to push boundaries and make trouble. Tears filled Laurie's eyes as he consoled her, saying, "It's OK, sweetie," while he handed her a Kleenex. He then turned to me and repeated the question. With all the courage I could muster and urgently feeling the need for the toilet again, I quietly murmured, "I think we should switch back and forth." Then all I could do was look down and let the fear from my betrayal consume me.

Laurie and I waited with Steve's assistant, Barbara, on the courthouse steps. Mom pulled the station wagon around; her face was a mask of politeness. She said thank you and quickly ushered us in the car. Underneath that calm façade was a woman boiling with anger. We could feel her fury radiating out like heat missiles, and I was the target. As if she knew I was the one who'd betrayed her.

The trip home was absolute silence. Terrifying, utter silence. Pressing my head against the car window, I watched the tree-lined streets of our neighborhood flash by as I dreamed of somehow escaping this nightmare. Mom sprayed gravel as she pulled into our driveway, slammed the car into park, and left us sitting there. Her ungrateful daughters, or perhaps just one daughter, who loved her father more.

In the days following, it was hard not to notice that Mom wasn't speaking to me. Laurie, on the other hand, would ask a question and Mom would immediately answer her. It was an emphasis of her distain for me at the time and an intentional, obvious denial of my existence. I was invisible. If only she knew how desperately I wanted to escape and actually *be* invisible. Laurie tried to console me, but what could she do? We were both pawns in the divorce, and from Mom's point of view the only loyalty we had, should be to her.

That week of silent treatment happened to coincide with my annual school picture day. Picture day was a big deal. Even in fifth grade, the peer pressure was overwhelming. I tried my best to put something super stylish together, which consisted of my favorite baby-blue satin jacket and my hair feathered back just like Farrah Fawcett's—high fashion at the time. The house was still and quiet when I finished prepping that morning, and the only thing left to do was ask Mom for picture money.

The hallway leading to my mother's room was dark, and I knew better than to turn on the light. Approaching her door with trepidation, I knocked, softly whispering, "Mom, are you awake?" Nothing. My heart pulsing in my ears, I knocked again a bit louder, "Mom, it's picture day. I need money." I waited. Still nothing. Not one sound. I sat down, unsure what I should do, inhaling the musty hallway smell. Maybe she just didn't hear me? *Knock louder.*

I got up and repeated my ask. I stood there alone in the silence. An hour prior to standing there, I was beaming with pride at my ability to put together a fashionable outfit without any help. Now all I felt was dejection. In one last attempt to get a response—any response—I knocked multiple times and loudly asked, "Mom, are you awake? I really need a little money, or I can't get my picture taken." Silence.

I finally realized she wasn't going to answer—she wasn't giving me money; I decided there was nothing else to do but leave. It felt like an elephant was sitting on my heart as I wiped the heavy tears from eyes. My mother had disowned me, or that's what it felt like. I had known there would be consequences for my betrayal, but never realized the price was so high. My neighbor's lights were slowly blinking on as I walked past on my way to school that early morning. I began chastising myself for opening my big mouth to the judge. *What were you thinking, you idiot?* Now my own mom had rejected me, and I would be the only kid unable to get a photo taken—certain to be the butt of everyone's joke.

When I arrived at school, I lied to my teacher and whispered that I'd forgotten to ask my mom for money. Mrs. Aguirre glanced up from her paperwork, took one look at me, and smiled. I'm not sure if she sensed something was wrong or saw how red my eyes were, but she immediately assured me it was alright and that other kids forgot money too. "You look so pretty today, Shaley," she said, "let's just get your picture taken and we'll worry about the money part later."

I'll never forget the tremendous relief I felt from that act of kindness. It was as if she knew, without actually knowing, that something was off. She had quietly safeguarded me from the humiliation of not being able to participate. Knowing I could still have a photo taken almost made me break down and sob. My classmates would never know—missing out on picture day would have been social death to a fifth grader. The pressure to fit in with my classmates was almost as stressful as my mother ignoring me. Almost.

The next time we were visiting Dad's, I realized he was also upset by the court's decision, even though it seemed to favor him. Actually, it wasn't the court's decision he was upset with; he was upset with Laurie.

Dinner at Dad's was the usual cacophony of overlapping conversations, interruptions, and laughter. Having three sisters on this side of the family, most discussions centered on hair, boys, and fashion. Yes, it was stereotypical, and usual until the conversation shifted to the courthouse. My stepmother, Geri, was clearing the table when Laurie innocently made the mistake of sharing her experience.

Dad interrupted her saying, "You did nothing."

Dad never got mad. He got perturbed occasionally, but never actually mad. I mean, he did seem to lose his shit once a year while trying to untangle the Christmas tree lights, but he'd never once took any anger out on us. Returning to the table, Geri broke the silence and reassured us, "Well, she did, Chuck. She showed up for both you and her mom," which was true.

Laurie's eyes swelled with tears. Out of all of us, she was the one who wanted Dad's approval the most. And Mom's. Don't get me wrong, we all wanted our parent' approval, but Laurie seemed to want it more. Maybe it was a middle child thing, I don't know. But it was clear his comment cut her deeply.

And what exactly was I supposed to do with all of this unstable back and forth behavior? My mind was once again swimming in a cesspool of confusion. At this house I was the hero. Abe Lincoln at one house, Benedict Arnold in the other. Deep sorrow consumed me, bordered with resentment and outrage. When I defended Dad, I lost Mom's approval. When Laurie didn't defend him, she lost Dad's approval. There was no winning the fucked up, twisted game forced upon us. We were unwilling participants, and it seemed it would never end.

FOUR

BABY BUTCH PROBLEMS

I sat around the kitchen table with my best friends, my second family really, laughing and munching on a family sized bag of potato chips. A bunch of 14-year-olds with no parents around and nothing better to do. A six-pack of Pabst Blue Ribbon sat quietly in the middle of the table, silently daring us to try one. Although consuming everyone's attention, we pretended to not notice it. Well, until Dave, straddling the kitchen chair backwards blurted, "I got it from my dad's stash," as he pointed to the beer, nearly falling backwards. Noticing the way he said "stash" made it seem like he had obtained highly coveted illegal drugs from the Mexican Cartel, not plain old beer. That, and the fact he didn't realize how loud he was talking, prompted a round of laughter from the group. Dave was the comedian of our gang. And though he tried to carry a tough-guy bravado, we all knew he was comic relief.

I could feel my arm hairs rise as a strange anticipatory static energy permeated the room. Glancing hesitantly back and forth at each other, we all wondered who would go first. Ignoring my inner voice, loud with trepidation, I broke the awkward silence, leaned over, and plucked a can off the plastic ring. The metal tab made a hissing sound as I pulled it open and took a big gulp. *Ew,* I thought as my eyes teared up. It was disgusting and it burned going down. All eyes on me, I swallowed the warm liquid and gave a loud adult-like belch, followed by a smirk. *It's all about appearances, baby, even amongst friends.* It tasted awful, like stale muddy water even a dog wouldn't drink.

Soon, all four of us had a can in our hands, pretending we were anything but kids. Within minutes we were giggling and giddy, feeling the warm liquid spread through our bodies. The pressures of our complicated teenage lives melted away. "Welcome to Fantasy Island!" Julie yelled, and we snorted with laughter. "The Plane! The Plane!" I replied, prompting more group laughter, while I cringed internally at my own sophomoric commentary. Luckily, we were all so completely self-absorbed in trying to outwit each other, my desperate need for acceptance wasn't too obvious. The irony of being a teenager; desperate to stand out and be a unique individual so the group will accept you.

After we'd finished the six-pack of beer that evening, I decided to skip all the way home. Yes, I literally skipped. It was dark and no one was around. But even if they were, I was pretty fucking tipsy and couldn't have cared less. My legs felt like rubber bands, each bounce taking me higher. If beer always made people feel so blissed-out and euphoric, I wanted it all the time. Moreover, it miraculously made my teenage anxieties disappear. And by "teenage anxieties" I don't mean schoolwork, or body image struggles, or peer pressure. I mean being a big, closeted lesbian.

No one in our entire school, and certainly no one in my inner circle of friends, was homosexual. The clear and overwhelming rhetoric was consistently about the heterosexual lifestyle. Being straight was the "normal" way of existing. Taking someone of the same sex to the prom for example would have been absurd. Understandable for me, the possibility of being exposed as a lesbian, given my surroundings, would've meant certain social death.

There was nothing, absolutely nothing, that scared me more than someone figuring out I was gay.

Homophobia permeated my world wherever I went. It was commonplace to hear degrading homophobic slurs and "jokes" casually intertwined with routine conversations. People using the word "faggot" or "ugly dyke" were common. And yep, 'ugly' was typically part of the verbiage "dyke or lesbo". What was shocking is how often I participated or laughed along. Almost as if I'd never considered the impact these words carried. *Wow, these jokes are really cruel and disparaging. Maybe I should stop?* Yet, I didn't stop. I continued to pretend I was straight and made sure I was never, ever seen defending anyone suspected of being gay. The obvious conclusion of course, was anyone defending someone's sexual orientation must be gay themselves. Anyone stepping outside of the heteronormative bubble, even slightly, was subject to any number of verbal, sometimes physical, attacks. I was living in a gay version of the Salem Witch trails. You'd better be careful, or you might be accused the moment you step out of line. I hated it, but I didn't write the rules. I just had to survive.

Our middle school PE teacher, Ms. Brown, was a constant target of our adolescent, homophobic jokes. Who knew if she actually was a lesbian? She definitely portrayed the stereotypical image of a masculine, sweat suit wearing, "big boned" woman who taught sports. And sports at the time were still very much dominated by men. So, duh, if you were a woman who enjoyed sports you were probably a dyke.

As soon as she was cast as lesbian, there was no coming back. She was forever framed as the manly, disgusting, lesbian PE teacher that ogled all the girls. We in turn would run to the locker room after class, laughing and shouting, "Hurry, before Ms. Brown comes in and checks out your naked butt!"

One day in open gym class, I watched a small group of girls deliberately lob their basketballs in her direction. She was sitting

on her folding chair looking down at paperwork when one finally connected with her face. I gasped, tearing up at the look of
stunned shock as she immediately grabbed her head in obvious
pain. Maybe in the moment, I recognized that Ms. Brown and I
were the same person, or perhaps it was just the universal empathy
we feel seeing another human in pain. No one noticed my reaction
and I quickly recovered, joining in the murmurs and side-giggles
that flooded the gym. I did nothing and said nothing. I wouldn't
dare or they'd come for me. The shame I felt from participating
in such callous and cruel behavior, even as an observer across the
gym, has never gone away.

Whether I was getting books out of my locker, raising my
hand in class, playing tetherball on the playground, or listening to
my coach at practice—my mind was always on guard duty, ready
to smack down anyone who thought I wasn't fully committed to
"team boys". Every once in a while, I'd even spout homophobic
slurs to make absolutely sure no one doubted me. "Fucking fag,"
I'd mumble at an unfortunate passerby, loud enough for my friends
to hear. I was reinforcing the idea that I wasn't one of "them."
Then we'd all laugh and bond over my disparaging comment. I
mean we were all just joking, right? *No one really gets hurt from gay
jokes—lighten up, Shaley.*

This is what I'd think, in a feeble attempt to convince myself
no harm was done, while internally fighting a rising sense of dis-
grace. I knew exactly what I'd done, not only to him, but to me.
I'd single handedly stabbed us both in the heart at the same time.
And then, as if nothing happened, I'd dismiss those self-conscious
thoughts and remind myself—no, insist—that it didn't matter.
Fucking toughen up, Shaley. I had to survive.

By that point in my life, fear had become my constant companion, shadowing me as I went about my teenage life. Every single thought lingered in the very real consequence of being ostracized and outcast if someone discovered my secret. No one was

openly gay in my world. If someone was ever thought to be gay, I'd hear about it third-hand or through gossip in a despairing manner. "Did you hear about Emily's uncle? Yeah, he's totally a fucking faggot." Pejorative comments about people I'd never met.

Whenever I hear people go on about how they would have, of course, stood up in a situation like this, one that challenges the authoritative norm of the time, I have to laugh. Whether it's the peer pressure of teenagers, a bully in the workplace, or being the only person to stand in front of an oncoming tank: everyone wants to believe they would have the courage to stand against the crowd. They would be the one person to proclaim, "This is wrong!" But when it comes down to it, not many people are that brave, at least not consistently. Yet we all have our moments of grace and courage. For me, even if I wanted to, I could never forget the times when I took the coward's way out, or the shame that followed. It would take years to be able to embrace, love, and forgive that scared part of me.

The summer after ninth grade, we had a once-in-a-lifetime opportunity to travel to Egypt and Saudi Arabia. Being a self-absorbed teenager, I of course complained the whole time, clearly lacking perspective. Let's see, hanging out with friends riding my bike around the neighborhood for three months or having a mind-blowing travel experience in the Middle East? Adult no-brainer. Yet my friends were sort of another surrogate family. Besides Laurie, they were my confidants. I shared everything with them. Well, everything except that I was super gay. So, from the perspective of a teenager, leaving them behind was a serious emotional hardship.

The trip of course was overall thrilling and broadened my horizons extensively. However, the overt sexism and the way women were treated was difficult to witness, even at my age. Women were clearly seen as objects to men. I literally saw a pickup pass by with goats—yes, goats—in the front cab while the women were hunched over, huddled in the bed of the truck.

One morning while we were staying at a hotel in Cairo, I was waiting alone for the elevator to head back to our room. I'm not sure why I felt OK being alone. Ignorance, perhaps? When the doors opened, the only other person inside was the operator who was of course, a man. As soon as the doors closed, he turned and proceeded to feel me up. His grotesque, large fingers were all over me. I was a young, naive teenager who barely even had tits, so I had no clue how I possibly could've been a turn-on. Again, my ignorance shining through. I was so frightened and stunned, I just stood there, frozen. I'd never experienced anything like that and honestly wasn't sure what was happening at the time. Then the elevator doors opened, and he said with a skin-crawling grin, "Thank you." I don't remember exiting the elevator or entering our hotel room, but I definitely remember my mom's face when she saw me.

In the time it took to walk from the elevator to our room, I didn't react at all. I was so young not to mention, didn't speak the language. I didn't know what to do. Technically I know what happened was sexual assault and today would be called out immediately. It was a different time period, and I didn't know to speak up. No one openly complained about being molested or assaulted. If they did it was rare because overall most cultures, and definitely Middle Eastern culture, allowed that behavior, often even encouraging it. "Oh, boys will be boys" or "You must have been wearing something sexy to provoke such attention." I was a flat chested 14-year-old. I didn't understand what had just happened was even wrong. I was completely naïve to the fact I had just been violated. I did know I'd never go into an elevator alone again.

"What happened?" Mom immediately asked upon seeing my face.

I mumbled through our exchange in a sort of dumbfounded haze, "The man in the elevator just felt me up."

"What?" she exclaimed, taking me in her arms.

As she pulled me tight, the trembling in my body heightened, as if knowing it was safe to let loose. It had stunned me and threw me off balance.

"Well, next time you just tell him you don't like men, you like girls." she said as she pulled me closer.

In a heartbeat, my trembling stopped and my body froze. *What was the likelihood she knew my little secret?*

That absolutely terrified me.

Suddenly, I was consumed with the possibility she knew my secret, which abruptly halted all thoughts of the elevator molester, shifting them into a hyper-focused fear of being outed. Even I could see how twisted and fucked up it was that a gross man had put his unsolicited grubby fingers on my body, and I was more worried about my mom knowing I was gay.

When I returned home that summer, I was sitting around drinking with my friends, because of course that's a normal activity 14-year-olds engaged in and told them what happened in the elevator. "Oh my God! That's gross!" they all said in unison. "What'd your mom say?" Feeling my face blush, I took a big gulp of beer, and lied. "Oh", she just said, "These men can't keep their hands off a pretty girl." "Ewwww," they groaned in solidarity.

The entire experience made me more committed to keeping up my straight girl façade, and this newly discovered liquid substance helped. It didn't take away my burgeoning sexual fantasies and desires for girls, but it sure numbed everything and pushed all fear down deep. I loved it. Strange that I'd welcome the prospect of denying myself the only thing I had ever wanted. But since there wasn't a fucking chance in hell that I was ever going to admit I was a lesbian; escaping was a major relief. A miracle, really. With the toxifying effects of beer, I began to actually think I could be normal, like everyone else.

Laurie, me and Dad. He always made us laugh and feel at home wherever we were.

Mom with me when I was one year old. Clearly very happy then. Also, I was a pudgy little kid.

My Mary Lou Retton
tomboy haircut,
thinking I was all
that and then some.

Believe it or not, I
did try hard on
school picture day

Laurie and me as
young kids. Come
on, it's seriously
cute.

Laurie and me as
adults. My
touchstone.

FIVE

GAYS, DRUGS, AND BLEEDING, OH MY!

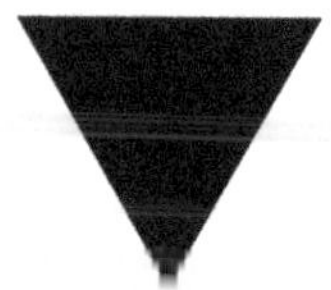

By the time I was 14, the fatigue from constantly feeling on guard began to sink in. Not a day went by where I didn't feel like the odd person out, paranoid someone would discover my secret. At times I fantasized I could just end it all, unable to see a way out. It was enough pressure to chip away at even the most resilient, ardent soul. My life was a broken record of, "Why don't you have a boyfriend? Are there any cute boys you're interested in? You sure hang out with a lot of girls. Is everything OK?" Girls liked boys and boys liked girls. There was no alternative.

My mind would instantly shift into overdrive when these questions were asked, as nervous energy flooded my body. A surge of panic happening internally while externally I forced myself to appear calm and collected, downplaying any hint of being homosexual. "Well, I play sports, so duh! Of course, I'm hanging out with lots of girls. You don't see co-ed sports teams, do you?" Always defensive and diverting these conversations to another subject. Any subject, as long as it wasn't about being gay.

Luckily my flawless, sporty girl, bouncing ponytail disguise, combined with my vigilance around defending any hint of being gay, worked like magic. I'd always secretly wondered, though, *How do they not see right through me?* It felt like I stuck out like a sore thumb, towering over people with my "big boned" body and androgynous face. I seemed so obviously gay. But people, it seemed, were oblivious. Like Superman, I supposed. I never understood how a simple pair of reading glasses disguised him. "Oh my God! Where did he go? Superman was just here!" All I had to do was wear a ponytail and act like a homophobic asshole. People saw what they wanted, or perhaps they chose to pretend not to notice the big butch lesbian in front of them.

Before puberty, I was indifferent when it came to whether I hung out with boys or girls. I couldn't have cared less. If someone was fun, we hung out. Before hormones started wreaking havoc on my body, I was able to compete on the same level athletically with boys—until I couldn't. In just one summer, my friend Scott had developed fucking supernatural strength and could hit a baseball past our outfielders, but my athletic ability stayed the same. I felt betrayed and defeated by my own body. We had always been equal, anything boys could do, I could do (often better, I might add). It wasn't that I wanted to be a boy, I just thought I'd always be able to compete with them physically. Apparently, that's not typically how it works. Without my consent, my body had taken on a life of its own.

Then everything fell apart. Early one morning, when I was around 15 years old, I woke up feeling my pajamas glued to my body. Something was wrong. I laid there with a pit in my stomach, sweating and hot, afraid to move. Suddenly I felt it. "What on earth is happening?" I yelled out loud to no one in particular. I rushed to the bathroom in a panic and saw gallons of blood everywhere. Well, maybe just one splotch, staining my once-clean tighty-whities.

Mind you, I wasn't completely naïve. I knew that girls bled, but I was shocked that it was happening to me. *A warning, people!*

How about some sort of warning! I internally screamed, sitting there with absolutely no clue what to do. My mental peanut gallery had all sorts of imaginative, immature, and crass commentary at the ready that typically would have cracked me up. But in that moment, all I felt was fear.

There was a girl in school whose mom actually threw her a menstrual party. A period party. In my world, menstrual parties were not the norm. Mom had hardly been around to cook us dinner or ask us about our daily lives, so it was pretty safe to assume we certainly never even had the "period" conversation. In all fairness to my mom, she did always remember our birthdays and threw us great parties, but a menstrual party?

When hearing of this, my friends exploded with laughter. "What does a period party look like?" I asked, "I mean, would there be piñatas with toilet paper and maxi-pads inside?" A friend then added, "And would they be covered in…." You get the picture. Yes, our maturity level was impressive. Right then, however, I sure could've used some sort of guidance. I was stumbling around aimlessly and desperate for help. If only there had been one of those cheesy *Afterschool Specials* about menstruation, something like "Sarah's Song: Now You're a Woman."

After shoving a wad of toilet paper into my pajamas, I waddled upstairs and sat in front of the heater. I felt strangely violated and broken. The warm air rushed over me and blanketed me in comfort. What would I tell everyone? Should I hide it? The agony of hiding one more thing sent a rush of panic through me. I was confused and teeming with anxiety.

When Mom emerged from her bedroom, I told her what had happened. It all felt like some weird confession, like I had accidentally broken my body. My crotch was fucking bleeding, so something did break, or broke loose, I supposed. She sighed and said, "Oh, honey, is that all?" I just stood there with my mouth agape, dramatically horrified in a way only a teenager could embody. *Se-*

riously? Is that all? There is blood coming out of my body and it's not a Band-Aid kind of problem, Mom!

Not long after that, came the accompanying increase in hormones, which was far worse than bleeding from my crotch. I felt like I was going insane. Not only did I feel bloated, sweaty, and stinky, but girls were constantly on my mind. My desire for other girls skyrocketed and pretending to be straight was almost unbearable. My desires and urges were crushing me. Until that point in my life, I hadn't fully accepted I was a lesbian. I knew I was different, but the term lesbian wasn't used much then. I suppose, at a bare minimum, I was confused. And prior to all this, even though drawn more towards girls, I certainly hadn't developed strong desires for either sex. Then the Niagara Falls of hormones hit and I turned into this sexual creature attracted to—no, obsessed with—the same sex. The wrong sex. It was paralyzing. This was much more perilous than any amount of menstrual blood.

My world overnight, had become even more complicated and confusing. To say I was tired would've been an understatement. An enormous amount of my energy was already focused on perfecting the believability of my straight girl facade and fending off anyone daring to question it. Now there was blood pouring out of my body and a new, unwanted escalating (borderline compulsive) tsunami of hormonal desires for the same sex.

I don't remember what I daydreamed about prior to hitting puberty. Maybe it was whether tater tots would be served at lunch the next day? Or how I could beat Bobby in the next game of wall ball. Whatever they had been before, my new daydreams were all about girls. Girls chasing me, actually. Almost every night, I'd lay in bed fantasizing about being Buck Rogers or Flash Gordon. I was a baby butch lesbian in the late 1970s, what were you expecting?

I'd picture myself zooming around in my badass ship, outfitted in a sexy full-body space suit, shooting my star blaster at the enemy. I have no recollection who the enemy was in those TV shows, but it didn't matter. My fantasies weren't about a faceless evil enemy trying to destroy everything, they were about being desired. I mean, I was Buck or Flash, and I was saving everyone. Who wouldn't want to chase "Flash Gordon, Savior of the Universe"? "Flash! You're amazing! Take me!" they'd scream, and I'd run away beaming with delight.

Yes, I would run away. I didn't know what was supposed to happen after they caught me. Were we supposed to hold hands? Kiss? I had no clue about straight sex, let alone gay sex. In my fantasy world, they'd desire me, catch me, then the whole thing would start over. It was a G-rated, young, closeted lesbian's version of fantasy tag. Some nights I'd switch up my story and suddenly I was Steve Trevor, washing up on Wonder Woman's island—an island populated only by women. But whether I was Flash, Buck, or Steve, we never got to the part where there was physical contact.

At some point, even my most vivid fantasies would begin to fade, and the reality of who and what I was would creep forward again. I'd cry silently in my bed, wondering why I was born gay. It's hard to convey the isolation and sheer loneliness of being closeted. I somehow knew it was never a choice, but I didn't understand why someone like me, so loving and sensitive, would be brought into such a cruel and unwelcoming world. I questioned whether I could ever have, or even deserve, someone who would love me the way I would love her.

Then I'd wake up the next morning, put on my cloak of homosexual invisibility, and continue on, pretending to like boys, trying to pass. In school, I'd linger in the hallways before class, sometimes hovering on the outskirts of the popular girl cliques, listening in, trying to appear inconspicuous and cool, as if part of the group. They'd be giddy with chatter about which boys they were crushing on and who they couldn't wait to kiss. All I could think of was how much I wanted to *be* those boys. Or Buck Rodgers.

It was a lazy afternoon, and no one was home. Laying on my bed, bored, I decided to rummage through my mom's medicine cabinet. Alcohol helped maintain my straight girl illusion and silence my anxieties so there was no particular reason at the time for such unauthorized behavior, except perhaps that I was a teenager with nothing better to do. I stood there, staring at the overflowing, translucent, amber-colored bottles crammed on the shelves. Curiously, I started examining each one, trying to decipher the confusing labels. There were so many. *Jesus, Mom, what's with all the medications?* I thought. *There's a pill for every problem here.*

As I scanned them, one large bottle filled with thick, white pills kept drawing my attention. "For pain," the label said, "Take 1-2 every four hours as needed." Twisting off the cap, I tapped out a pill and considered my options. "Vi-co-din," I sounded out. *Just one can't hurt*, I thought as I rolled the fat chalky pill around in my palm. At the time, they all looked exactly alike to me: mostly white in color and round or oval in shape. It was hard to tell them apart. Who knew that years later, I would develop a strange mutant superpower, able to identify what kind of pills were in a bottle 20 fucking feet away? Not something to brag about, I guess.

I downed the pill with a can of Shasta and laid there for a few minutes, body tingling with anticipation. The next thing I knew, Jefferson Airplane was belting out "White Rabbit" and the walls of my room started to melt. No, of course that didn't happen. It was a pain killer, not an LSD-induced psychedelic trip. I was, however, consumed with an energetic bliss that permeated every pore of my body. It—no—*I* felt like heaven. I jumped up and started dancing on the bed, gyrating back and forth like Madonna screeching, "Holiday!"

Just one of those beautiful pills made me feel warm and weightless, without a care in the world. It was love at first sight. They masked any physical pain I was experiencing while also eliminating all emotional and mental concerns. Alcohol had numbed me but fucking Vicodin instantly erased any and all of my teenage anxieties. Not to mention the euphoria, the heavenly euphoria!

At the time, getting Vicodin wasn't easy. Alcohol, on the other hand was easy to get. And since it was everywhere, by default it ended up as our preferred drug of choice. But we didn't call it a "drug". It was just beer, and all the cool kids drank it. Beer made every social gathering, big or small, a serious party. Getting wasted at a beer kegger made you part of the in-crowd. Bonus points to your cool credibility if the cops busted a party you attended. "Dude, did you see how wasted everyone was at the kegger Saturday before it got shut down? So rad!" No one talked about the painkillers they scored, just how everyone was falling down drunk from alcohol. Always keeping it classy.

Even if I did manage to score throughout my teen years, any noticeable side effects from my emerging pill addiction were completely eclipsed by my increasingly regular drunk state of being. If I was slurring words or nodding off from narcotics, I could easily pretend it was just the effects of alcohol and no one was the wiser. The insidious, more covert nature of opioid addiction wasn't as obvious as the blatant side effects that came from drinking. Plus, this was the mid-1980s, when most people had no clue popping pain killers was a growing problem.

Being an addict or alcoholic back then was viewed similarly as being a homosexual. Both were seen as abnormal, even repulsive, behaviors that people intentionally *chose* to partake in. The problem was that the continual political and social narratives most people believed, was riddled with ignorance and often cemented in uncompromising religious morals. The general public was sorely lacking any basic understanding or scientific knowledge around the disease of addiction, sexual orientation, and what it meant to be gay in America. And since there weren't many mainstream conversations about being gay or addiction, at least nothing positive, both were judged and ignored, in hopes these eyesore "problems" of America would simply fade away.

But addiction doesn't simply go away, and it moves at a different pace for every addict. The end result, however, is usually the same. Picture yourself on the outer edges of a tornado where you hardly detect any change in air pressure. You think you're safe at a distance, observing, enjoying the thrill of it all, feeling your body tingle from the electricity in the air. Then you notice you're slowly being pulled inward, towards the center of the storm. Before you know it, your head is pounding, feeling like it will implode any second from the pressure. You're fully aware that you're too close and need to turn back but you can't seem to control your own body. Panic seizes you and you realize it's too late. Years pass like minutes and you're at the mercy of the tornado, being tossed around with flying cows, Dorothy, and memories of the life you once had.

SIX

GET OUT

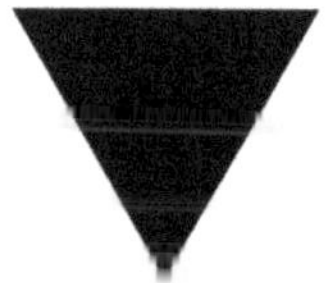

I know I wasn't exactly the easiest teenager but really, do "easy" and "teenager" ever belong together? I was just entering my sophomore year in high school after moving, again, to a new home. The stresses of moving, being closeted, and entering a brand-new school when you're 15 felt like near death on the teen drama scale. My, "I have absolutely no control" list just kept growing.

Trying to fit in, I decided to join a variety of sports, which I quickly discovered gave me a sense of place. It was almost like a second home, or in my case third, since I lived with my mom but also had my dad's. Playing team sports, I was accepted and excelled, particularly in soccer and basketball. Softball was just something I rolled into because it came after basketball. I mean, there was nothing else to do, so why not tag people out at first base?

Funny, out of all the stereotypical lesbian sports, softball was number one. Yet I only reluctantly joined out of boredom. The only other option for spring sports was track. Coach Bob wanted me badly for shot put. *I'd have to give that one a big thumbs down, Bob.* If I wanted to keep my covert straight girl image, there wasn't a snowball's chance in hell I was going to be the big woman hurling a shot put. Back in the early 1980s? You might as well call me

Helga and put me on the East Germany Olympic women's team. Talk about stereotypes. No thank you.

You'd think being a closeted baby dyke, playing sports with a lot of other girls might be difficult, or at bare minimum, hormonally challenging. But it turned out, it made life easier. Growing up with all sisters I was inherently more comfortable around females, gay or straight. Plus, blending in was a piece of cake since most of the players looked similar to me with a universal sporty ponytail. Who knows how many "sisters" were in the locker room with me back then?

"Doogie!" my teammate Shannon yelled when I entered the locker-room. This was a loving nickname given to me after a team trip to the coast. I had mistakenly referred to sand buggies as sand "doogies" in my sleep deprived head, cracking my teammates up and forever earning me the nickname "doogie." I dramatically rolled my eyes hearing her, yet internally bubbled over with delight. Even though I was filled with nervous butterflies in anticipation of our game that afternoon, there was also a certain internal calm and safety I felt when hanging with my teammates. I was amongst family. Despite the homophobic world that seemed to surround me everywhere else, when with my teammates, I didn't feel as much pressure to conform. I belonged to something for the first time in my life and felt a genuine connection and camaraderie. My coaches and teammates seemed to really like me, not just because I was a good athlete but as it turned out, I was a pretty likable person.

Too bad I was also rather fucked up emotionally. Anyone paying close attention could have seen right through my "nothing fazes me" exterior to the scared little girl inside, hurting. But again, we weren't really programmed then to speak openly about problems. Yes, shit happened around us and to us constantly, but we either kept it to ourselves or made jokes—lots of jokes.

My heart continued to ache and long for someone to love me. Every day seemed like déjà vu, a never-ending cycle of trying to fit in and find a community of people who accepted me. Even with my sports family, there was really no one to open up to. Just the thought of confiding in anyone about being gay prompted a panicky, "No, absolutely no, no, no, no, absolutely *not*." Plus, I was a teenager. What teenager, especially back then, had conversations with friends about loneliness and fitting in?

To say I was resentful towards my mother would have been the understatement of the year. Her unpredictable behavior and inconsistent messages of love left me on edge and questioning my self-worth. One minute, she'd praise me, the next ignore me, and the next scold me. And she was a master of manipulation. "Well, at least the cat will keep me company tonight," she once muttered casually as I was heading out the door to meet friends. My throat constricted as I fought the urge to respond. I knew better, well, usually knew better, so kept walking. There was no winning. She didn't want our company, just control. Laurie and I often joked if there were ever a contest for guilt tripping, she would've been crowned queen. Her treatment of us was highly dependent on her moods, and as a result, by the age of 15, I had learned to be suspicious of not only *her* motives, but everyone around me.

Still preoccupied with my father and the divorce, she found every chance she could to remind us of how he had ruined everything. It had been a solid 10 years by that point and my father was happily remarried, living in a house in the west hills. I'm sure his genuine happiness only deepened her resentment and pain. She had spent years tormented by past socioeconomic inadequacies, always trying to prove her worth to the world, my dad, and his extended family. And in her eyes at least, I'm sure felt like a failure. Her second marriage to Larry had been tumultuous from the start and she soon became estranged from him while he lived and worked thousands of miles away in Saudi Arabia.

The thing is, as much as I loved my mom despite our complicated relationship, none of her problems were my fucking fault. I was drowning in my own teenage cauldron of unmanaged emotions, and the one person who was supposed to lovingly guide me through these struggles, wasn't there. With no one to turn to, each day seemed like a battle just to keep the emptiness, confusion, and isolation inside from consuming me. Or worse, morphing into explosive anger. Anytime I'd feel a wave of heat roll through me, I'd mentally tell myself, "You're fine, Shaley. Just chill. Think about something else." To outsiders, I'm certain I appeared like any typical, awkward, good-natured teenager—always acting laid-back and aloof. But underneath, I was embarrassed about my homelife and ashamed I was gay. And my growing awareness of the unfair nature of it all incensed me. I was a terrified imposter living a lie.

One afternoon Tina, Jill, and I were downstairs watching TV. The three of us would often hang out after practice, most of the time with no one else in my house, just laughing and screwing around. We all played the same sports, had the same class schedules, and made sure our lockers were right next to each other. We were the three musketeers. "All for one! One for all!" Unless of course it came down to talking about personal emotional issues or serious family problems. Then it was tumbleweeds blowing in the wind.

Our friendship *was* genuine, though. We were just products of our environment—never shown or taught how to express ourselves in a healthy way. In fact, the messages we received were to "toughen up" and push through whatever was physically or mentally happening at the time. Instead of talking about our feelings or experiences, we were literally told to "buck up buttercup" more often than not. All of us had home lives that on some level, were fraught with difficulties. Yet because we didn't understand how to cope and handle these problems effectively, we pretended nothing unusual was happening. We dealt with our emotional pressures and problems the only way we knew how. We ignored them and preoccupied ourselves by goofing around, laughing a lot, and playing sports. Lots of sports.

Tina was talking about her older sister and the argument they had that morning about clothes. Apparently, like Laurie and me, they stole each other's clothing without asking too. I knew firsthand it was a big deal. Jill made a joke about Tina's sister stretching out one of Tina's favorite shirts and we all burst out laughing. Suddenly from upstairs we heard, "Dammit, keep it down!" We froze—wide eyes shifting back and forth, unsure what to do. We thought maybe Laurie was home but didn't realize Mom was too. After a moment of agonizing silence, Tina and Jill stood up and started to leave. They had occasionally seen the unpredictability of my mom's behavior and I'm guessing wanted no part of it. "Come on, you guys, the show's not over. Just stay," I urged. But they both said they needed to get home soon for dinner. I knew they did not need to get home but didn't argue. Tina gave me a warm hug goodbye. It was the kind of hug that said, "I love you, friend. Hang in there." But of course, that wasn't openly shared.

I never knew if Mom would be in a good or bad mood, so part of me was OK with them leaving. It wasn't worth the embarrassment of her coming down and snapping at us more for laughing too loud or possibly just taking up space. "OK, I'll see you guys tomorrow at school," I said trying to hide my shaking voice as I closed our front door. I turned and yelled, "They're gone! Are you happy?!" Then I ran to my room, tears threatening to fall and muscles quivering as I reflexively hit my wall as hard as I could. Slamming my door, I sank down to the carpet, alone in the silence, not seeming to notice my knuckles beginning to swell.

With Mom's unpredictable moods and my ever-growing, *very* predictable teenage resentment, tensions started to become unbearable between us. Inevitably one day, our volatile interactions merged into the perfect storm, and it all blew. "I hate you so much!" I yelled as I slammed my door—again. This time she followed in her own rage yelling, "Get out! You go live with him. You go live with Chuck!" The funny thing is, I don't remember what we were fighting about. It could have been about coming home late, or hanging out with friends she didn't approve of, or maybe I ate the last of the ice cream, who knew? It didn't matter. The anger I felt towards her in that moment had been festering for a long time, and it was pure venom spewing out of me.

Hand shaking, I picked up the landline and dialed my dad. I was doing my best to remain stoic, but the moment he answered the phone my voice cracked. "Dad? Can…can you come get me?" His answer was immediate and without question. I waited alone on our concrete porch in the autumn nighttime air. I had stuffed my school supplies, soccer uniform, and cleats for our match the next day in my duffel bag, which I slumped over, motionless. I could hear Laurie's muffled voice upstairs trying to reason with Mom as I stared off in the distance with glassy eyes, my face seemingly made of stone.

Dad pulled up and promptly embraced me. I trembled as I sank into his arms, unsure how to respond. Geri did her best to keep the conversation cheery on the drive to their house, sure to avoid any questions about what had happened. A wave of dumfounded shock moved through me, numbing my ability to form any coherent thoughts or sentences. But her attempts at levity were greatly appreciated.

As I made my way up to the spare bedroom, the emotional weight of what had happened left me exhausted. Finally, alone after hugging goodnight, I managed to set my bag on the dresser before melting into the bed. Then I felt the tickle of Lilly, Geri's small, curly-haired dog next to me, trying to nuzzle up. She let me sob silently into her fur, turning to lick my cheeks occasionally. I've always wondered if perhaps animals are from some other realm, sent here to show us pure unconditional love. I know the fur of dogs and cats I've owned over the years have definitely soaked up countless tears.

The following morning at school, Tina came up to my locker and asked, "What happened? I called your house last night and your mom said you no longer lived there." I replied with a nonchalant detached sigh, "Yeah, I decided I wanted to live with my dad who's being super cool and wants me to stay with him." Even though Tina would have understood, opening up never seemed like a safe option. If there was one thing I'd learned for certain; people could change their feelings and minds in a heartbeat. Friends, family, teachers—it didn't matter. The world I had been shown was one where people weren't always trustworthy. It was best, and usually easier, to keep everyone at a distance and not reveal much. But my close friends weren't dumb or naive. They knew my history and struggles with my mom and the divorce. Seeing right through my tough guy front, Tina kindly decided to let it go. "Your dad is awesome," she said giving me a slight hug and proceeded to change the subject.

Later on, Jill's mom dropped me off at my dad's house after our game. I was feeling fairly stable and upbeat, having spent the day distracted by school and friends. I always felt energized and content playing sports. Whether on the soccer field or basketball court, I was able to zone out and escape: a temporary reprieve from my problems. I walked into the living room and almost tripped over Lilly's joyful greeting of, "Oh my God, where have you been all day—I missed you!" As I bent down to pet her, the somber atmosphere in the room hit me. I couldn't tell exactly what had happened, but over the years I had learned how to detect the slightest shift in energy around adults. Almost like a sixth sense, my muscles would tighten, and eyes and ears shift into high alert, scanning my surroundings for whatever, or whoever, posed a danger. It was like a predator/pray defensive strategy, that would immediately shut all doors of vulnerability.

"Hey," I tentatively said to both Dad and Geri, who were sitting in their matching armchairs. "Hey, Sha," Dad said, "come sit down." The pit in my stomach dropped as I wondered if there would ever be a day in my life without some level of anxiety. With teary eyes he said, "We love you, honey, but we can't have you here. It's complicated and has nothing to do with you. We love you very much." My heart collapsed as panic poured into my extremities. What I heard him say was, "We all know this is a game for your mom and she doesn't really want you here. She just wants to hurt me, and I can't handle it anymore. You are expendable."

I knew on a deeper level that wasn't true. Even though his words and actions were contradictory, my dad did want me there. But after years of being on my mother's emotional rollercoaster ride, the fatigue from it all was sinking in. I felt like I didn't belong anywhere. Not even at Dad's house.

In hindsight, my father was likely dealing with more legal threats from my mother. I was still considered a minor so couldn't simply move to my dad's without the courts stepping in. Even though she technically kicked me out, it could have been another litigious nightmare. The court system back then leaned heavily in favor of mothers in divorce situations, giving them much more leverage and power. And my father, who fought extremely hard for us, was frustrated that the custody agreement had been so one-sided.

Geri shared years later that the judge had bluntly stated his opinion that girls were better off with their mother, no matter the desires or abilities of their father, so long as there was no actual physical abuse involved on the mother's side. Emotional instability and abuse were apparently acceptable or ignored. None of this surprised me. Hell, this was the same system that pitted Laurie and me against our own parents' years prior, pressuring us to decide the fate of Christmas visitations. The court system was skewed and ignorant when it came to what was truly best for the children.

For my mom, exercising what little control she did have in her life was another game. In reality, demanding I move out had nothing to do with me or what I was going through. She never seemed to want to understand why her daughter was so angry and upset. Or perhaps did care on some level but didn't want to dive deeper. It was easier to send me over to Chuck's as punishment. But it wasn't punishment—I loved my dad and would've lived there. Unfortunately, we all knew if I had tried to stay, it would have led to more chaos and pain.

As they drove me back to Mom's, there was no cheery conversation, just silence. I hadn't cried yet and dammit I wasn't going to. *Keep it together, Howard,* I thought. As we pulled up, the streetlights were just starting to flicker on, and shadows crept through the neighborhood. The house was completely dark and, not surprising to me, the front door was locked. I audibly sighed a laugh of resignation when I tried the doorknob thinking, "Oh course. This fucking nightmare will not end." I told Dad and Geri I'd be right back as I ran around the house, looking for entry. Finally finding an open window, I slid inside and made my way upstairs. The hallway was barely visible except for a beam of yellow light coming from underneath the bathroom door. Hearing the fan, I knew she was in the tub.

Mom glanced up as I opened the door, appearing annoyed, as if I was interrupting her bath time. Laying down her book she sighed, "I'm glad you're home, honey. I hope you learned your lesson," not even acknowledging the fact we all just took a trip to fucking crazy town. I stood there awkwardly in the door frame; head pounding, and fists clenched trying to contain myself. My throat constricted as I fought the urge to scream. I was consumed with anger but knew I should continue staring at the floor. If I made eye contact, the fury I was barely able to contain, would have flooded the room. I forced a, "Yep," and closed the bathroom door.

Back out in the hallway, I fumbled for a light switch. When I went to unlock the front door, the porch light startled Dad and Geri, but I could see their relief. "Oh, honey, there you are!" Geri said. "Yeah, I knew a way in and talked to Mom. Everything's fine," I said briskly, not wanting to make eye contact, fearing a floodgate of tears. Dad just stood there looking at me through watery eyes. I will never forget the look of deep regret and anguish on his face as he said goodbye.

Watching them leave, a wave of sorrow blanketed me. I ran to the park, as I did often, looking for solace from nature and searching for "God." Yes, another dead-end talk with "God" or the universe, or whoever. The thing was, no one God or "spiritual being" had ever answered my calls for help. Can you be considered a lunatic at 15? I'm sure that's what I looked like, carrying on an apparent two-sided conversation through tears, and yelling at no one in particular.

I never understood what was so damn hard about answering. What's with all the bullshit religious "God loves you" rhetoric when he always seems to be conveniently absent? I was tired of platitudes like, "We must be patient and wait for a sign," or, "God speaks to us in mysterious ways," or the classic, "The universe only gives us what we can handle." You're the almighty, omnipresent, powerful creator of everything, right? Would it really have be that hard to simply answer my questions? Preferably in English. What was with all the cryptic, "riddle me this" religious crap? If you, God, created not only the Earth, but the universe and beyond, my teenage problems weren't that big of a deal to figure out. Hell, you could've fixed all my problems before breakfast.

I sat underneath a massive oak tree in a bed of dry leaves, crying, longing for someone, anyone, to simply see me, perhaps accept me for who I am, and fucking love me. "Am I really that unlovable?" I thought. I kept thinking there was no way I could possibly be the only person in the world unworthy of love. My mind bounced back and forth with a volley of grief and anger, then self-loathing and confusion. I'd been trying for years to contain my emotions, but things were spiraling. The reality of my life was catching up. No matter how much I screamed, cried, tried to fit in, looked for acceptance, or pretended I was someone else—I still woke up every day as me. A big, closeted lesbian in a broken family.

SEVEN

LESBIANS!

My head was throbbing when Tina dropped me off on campus that morning for the SAT's. I'm fairly certain I was still a little drunk from all the partying we'd done the night before. Yes, we drank and partied the night before taking what most people consider a monumental, life-changing test. *Yeah, you don't have a drinking problem, Shaley.* I gave the proctor a casual nod as I tried slinking unnoticed to the back of the classroom. He grimaced judgmentally as I passed, smelling the alcohol that permeated and clung to my clothing. "Take a seat anywhere. We're just about ready to begin." he said with unveiled condescension. I found a seat and stared down with bloodshot eyes at the intimidating, stark white test. "OK begin," I heard. Then with an audible sigh reflecting both my physical and mental state, I picked up my pencil.

Somehow, I shockingly passed with a score high enough that, along with my past decent grades, still gave me a few viable university options. I should have been elated when I received the news but felt indifferent. I was so lost already in life, unsure who I was, completely in the closet, and barely feeling like I fit in anywhere. The idea of having some masterplan for college and life seemed surreal and borderline ridiculous. "Meh. I guess I did OK." I told Tina almost apathetically when she asked how it went. My guardian angel must have been fed up by that point—I could picture the conversation with God, "Look, I'm serious. She is out of control, and I'm done. There's no reasoning with her, your grace." Guardian angel problems, perhaps.

I decided to become a duck at the University of Oregon. I loved ducks! Plus, Laurie was also attending U of O so it wasn't a hard choice. I am well aware most people, when choosing a university put *much* more effort into their decision process than, "I love ducks". But I unfortunately was still preoccupied with filling in and a host of other anxieties. Almost as if any higher functioning, frontal lobe brain activities were continually eclipsed and pushed aside by my reptilian brain, focused solely on surviving life.

Being a star basketball player in high school and thinking I was *all that and then some*, I decided I'd try out for the university women's basketball team. I walked in the day of tryouts wearing a cocky bravado only a naive eighteen-year-old could manage complete with chewing gum, smirk, and puffed out body. I had no clue what I was getting myself into. "Pssshhhhst, I got this," I thought hearing the familiar sounds of bouncing balls as I opened the gym door.

I momentarily froze when my eyes fixated on a giant woman occupying the court. I watched her glide gracefully skyward, easily touching the rim of the hoop, her long brown mane of a ponytail floating behind her as she soared. Up until that point, I'd only seen men jump that high so I stood there, gawking, mouth wide open like a baby bird.

To my surprise, I made the team. However, my enthusiasm and confidence collapsed when I realized rather quickly that the majority of the players were operating *far* beyond my skill level. They had players recruited from all over the world who towered over me. When we scrimmaged, they easily knocked down any feeble attempt I made at approaching the basket, let alone getting a shot off. I had been a formidable center post player in high school and was suddenly thrust into playing a guard. Making the team was impressive to most outsiders but really, I was on the third-string, "punching-bag" team. We were the expendable players that the starters ate for lunch. Trying to compete with them was like "my little pony" racing with a herd of thoroughbred stallions.

Running a half-court drill one afternoon with all three coaches triangulated around the court, whistles hanging from their lips—I passed the ball to the point guard then ran down to the paint to post up. I was trying to impress them. With what I wasn't sure. At a bare minimum I was working extraordinarily hard *not* to hear the whistle blow while I had the ball. Like a game of musical chairs, not wanting to be the one without a chair when the music stops, or in this case, holding the ball when the whistle blew.

Unfortunately, old habits die hard, and I still did not understand my place on the team. I turned and threw my hand up as I'd done a hundred times in high school, my back to the basket and yelled for the ball as I posted up. Given the superior basketball skills of the other players, the last thing I should have wanted was the ball, especially right at that moment. Why? Because behind me stood Trisha, or "T the Tank" as she was so lovingly called. She was only 5'10" but had a body built like a thick oak tree. A solid, impenetrable tree trunk.

Regrettably, I *was* successful in having the ball thrown to me, but completely unable to move the "tank". I forced all my energy into my leg and core muscles, tightening and squeezing as I tried repeatedly to hold my position. Rocking left and right, bobbing up and down, trying to out-maneuver her and perhaps slip by her side. But everything I tried, failed. She was too strong and comically seemed almost annoyed. As if I was a fly buzzing around her while she read the morning paper.

A piercing sound suddenly filled the gym as all three coaches simultaneously blew their whistles. My muscles were exhausted and shaking from struggling so long against the "tank" that I was grateful for the break but also nervous to see if *I* was the reason we stopped. I looked up at Trisha, my lungs burning, hands on my knees as I tried to catch my breath. I smiled as if we were sharing some teammate bonding moment we'd laugh about later with a look of, "That was great, right?" She glanced down at me almost as if noticing me for the first time, then looked away. The coaches briefly huddled together, then literally decided to use me as an example of how *not* to post up. The only thing I had going for me in that moment was it was impossible to determine if my face was bright red from embarrassment or physical activity.

With the combination of my continued problematic drinking, poor grades, mixed with my let's just say, "lack of contribution to my new team," it's weird I only lasted two terms at the University of Oregon. I dropped out and decided perhaps a community college might be a better fit both for my basketball skill level and let's face it, maturity level. So, I became a Penguin at Clark Community College. Yes, I went from being a terrifying Duck to a terrifying Penguin. Since I always fouled so much in basketball games, it seemed appropriate I had ended up as another fowl.

For a while, life seemed fairly good. Well, sort of. I excelled at basketball and felt a strong comradery with my fellow players. I, unfortunately, also continued to excel at drinking. I'm actually surprised that with all the falling down partying I did, I still managed to pass my classes and play decent basketball. As it turned out, my two years playing ball there were solid enough to grab the attention of a few four-year universities.

The recruitment process was basically an all-out wooing to persuade me to sign on with their school. This meant, "Show Shaley a good time so she'll come here." I'd fly into a university, and the coaches would greet me with such exaggerated enthusiasm I thought for sure they had misread my bio. I'd then get a campus tour, usually highlighting their state-of-the-art athletic facilities, followed by some elaborate dinner.

Like clockwork, as we finished eating, a few members of the basketball team would come by pretending to "save me" from the mind-numbing parents, "Oh my God, you must be so bored! It's time we show you how fucking fun this school really is!" Each time, I'd end up at some party. There were always parties and they always had alcohol. It's strange how accepted drinking was on college campuses, especially since most of the time we were underage. The burgeoning alcoholic in me loved it, "Why yes, I will have another pint, thank you."

This wasn't just one university. Every college that recruited me welcomed me with the same level of enthusiasm, like a pissing contest of who could "out-party" whom. At the University of Idaho, the level of drinking was off the charts. Also, if you weren't aware, the university is located in the city of "Moscoooh," Idaho, not Moscow. It was very important to differentiate the pronunciation, I quickly learned. Everyone I met, drank like fishes; I'm guessing out of boredom. There wasn't a whole heck of a lot to do in Idaho but drink and pretend you're somewhere else. I'm sure some people loved it, but for me, all I saw was never-ending hills filled with cows, cow smells, and more cows. Did I mention cows?

When I arrived, the first thing that hit me was the odor. Well, and heat. "Ugh what is that pungent smell?" I thought as I exited the plane, sweat already beading up on my forehead. The combination of warm weather and cow manure permeated everything. There was no escaping it, even indoors. It seemed to be alive. A living entity that attached itself like some 1950's movie about an alien blob impossible to remove once it leeched on to you.

Driving towards campus, in the politest tone I could muster, I asked coach Melissa, "Hey, so what's with the serious cow smells?" With a blank face, she looked back as if I asked her to solve an advanced calculous problem. "What smell?" she replied. As first impressions go, that was weird. But I decided not to push it and instead discreetly plug my nose until it hopefully passed. After a brief time, however, I understood. They had become desensitized. As if their senses had been severely dulled somehow. In only a matter of hours, my senses too seemed to acclimate, and I no longer smelled it. Well, as much. In reality, my senses most likely had kicked into survival mode, deadening and blocking my sense of smell temporarily.

Though externally no one could tell I was shaking, internally I was a continual tremoring earthquake of nerves. Simply being flown to a variety of universities was enough to tie up my stomach. It was exciting to be noticed but it was also stressful. The playful butterflies in my stomach more often felt more like angry hornets. I might have found more humor in the situation if balancing the two emotional extremes hadn't had me running to the bathroom so often. Throw in being closeted and I was a walking mess. Yet most people couldn't tell. I had mastered the art of "never letting them see you sweat" for years, knowing it was life or death if someone discovered my secret.

I was about to toss Idaho into the "absolutely not" bin, when I discovered their *complete* offer. It was one that, well—was impossible to refuse. "Yes, we know we have a cow smell 'issue' but if you sign with us today, Shaley, you'll not only get a full ride scholarship, all the partying and beer you want, but we will throw in…*lesbians!*" Yeah, I soon discovered the lesbians. Moscoooh, Idaho—with its never-ending rolling hills of cows, apparently also had lesbians. Out of all the colleges that were actively recruiting me, the answer was obvious. Of course, I'd choose Idaho. In a state full of cows, I had found the "golden calf". In the closet or out, Idaho had lesbians. You can't dangle the one thing I'd longed for my entire life in front of me and think I wouldn't bite.

I could hear the thumping bass before we even pulled up to the party. Getting out, I casually wiped the nervous sweat from my brow and followed the other women inside. With lightning speed, I was able to scan the crowd for other possible closeted lesbians. They were everywhere. And just as closeted as me it seemed. I quietly exhaled a deep sigh of relief. I was safe from being exposed. What a strange relief it was that no one else was out. The idea of coming out myself, or somehow being outed, terrified me, so oddly it did feel safe. "Head's up!" someone shouted, and a cold beer was thrown my way, condensation from the bottle hitting my skin. Given I was being recruited for my athletic abilities, I luckily caught it. "Thanks!" I shouted back, casually wiping the water from the bottle off my hand. Then I cracked it open and motioned a "cheers" to the group.

I was filled with a flurry of titillating exhilaration edged with terror surrounded by so many similar looking women. A clash of sorts was taking place internally, battling a lifetime of conditioned societal protocol. Mixed messages fluctuated between overwhelming surges of excitement and possibility, and fear of letting go. The air heavy with anticipatory static electricity, sent a wave of goose bumps down my body. My internal voice of reason, always fighting for control, started to remind me, well actually started screaming at me, to fucking dial it down and relax.

When a player asked me if I wanted another beer, I acted like a kid paralyzed on the first day of school. My heart was pounding so loud in my ears, I didn't even hear her. "Hey," she said, touching my arm gently, breaking me out of my daze. "You OK?" she asked quietly. Realizing I was just standing there, unable to breath, frozen with both trepidation and hidden desire, I quickly snapped out of it. Shaking my head, I said, "Yeah…. yeah. Sorry! Just off in la la land apparently." Then shrugged a laugh.

Fortunately, my initial shock soon melted away as alcohol worked its magic. Loosening everything up and of course, repressing any apprehension. For the first time in my entire life, women flirted with me. I mean, it was still all secretive and covert, but happening none-the-less. A tall woman with long auburn hair came over and introduced herself by sharing her name and position on the team. "Hi! I'm Kathy and I play post!" Looking up at her warm brown eyes, I suddenly felt exposed by her forward nature, confidence and beauty. My pupils dilated and face burned red as my body temperature immediately skyrocketed. Yes, I make the best first impressions. "So, you're the star recruit from Oregon?" she said. But it wasn't a question. It was an invitation.

Most people experienced with *any* level of flirting might have charmingly winked and smiled coolly saying, "Well, I am from Oregon but not sure about being the *star* recruit. Nice to meet you 'Kathy the Post'." But this is not how I responded of course. I began to laugh quietly at nothing, absolutely nothing. And I couldn't make eye contact. I just stood there, peeling the label off my beer bottle nervously.

Finally, my peanut gallery, who'd been oddly silent through the whole cringe-worthy interaction shouted, "Introduce yourself and stop laughing! Nothing is funny!" I wiped my copiously sweaty hands on my jeans and tried to stifle my nervous laugh. I then shot my right arm out with hand straightened in some sort of formal handshake position, as if we were about to agree on a landmark business deal. "I'm Shaley from Oregon," I blurted out quickly. My peanut gallery was slapping their foreheads in disbelief. Could I be anymore awkward? But then a smile broadened her face, and she chuckled taking my hand in hers, playfully shaking it comically up and down, making us both laugh. "Nice to meet you, Shaley from Oregon."

There were other women who floated in and out of flirtatious conversations with me that night, always trying to disguise their true intent. But the more alcohol consumed by everyone, the less subtle their advances and my response became. One even kissed me. Kissed me! A short, quiet kiss but still, a kiss. For someone who'd dreamed of kissing another woman all of her life, my heart was beating like a humming-bird's wings.

I knew after that, I was teetering on the edge of outing myself, moving from a life of strictly fantasizing about women to a world where I actually kissed one. A strange sort of purgatory almost— damned if I proceeded, damned if I did nothing. I could continue to suffer heartbreaking longings by not participating or give into to my overwhelming desires and risk it all. One choice meant a lifetime of miserable isolation, and the other meant being ostracized and socially rejected. Not a real win-win for "Shaley from Oregon." But given the extreme homophobia of the time, combined with the fact I was in Idaho, -(a state that wasn't exactly known for its progressive attitudes toward outsiders), I came to the decision I was much safer remaining in the closet.

To be a fly on the wall watching us would have been extraordinarily entertaining. I'm sure much of our lewd behavior came from our inebriated mental state, making it hard to maintain our outward, "No stop! I really do like men," disguise. But there was also an innate silent and secret language we shared that needed no alcohol to be understood. Some called it "gaydar." I felt it when I first walked through the door and instinctively nodded subtly, and of course with apprehension, at a few women at the party. It wasn't sexual, more of a quiet acknowledgment of others who shared the same secret. Whatever it was, it was real. It was embedded in our psyches and made it possible to pick up a signal of who was, and who wasn't, on our team. *Go "team" Idaho!*

On the plane ride home, I cringed thinking how we acted like prepubescent children in adult bodies, awkwardly stumbling around, touching, and sneaking kisses like a game of tag. Laughing hysterically at immature jokes while trying to maintain a suave, sexy, mature appearance. By this time in my life, many of my straight friends had not only found love but were even making wedding plans. Not me. I was practically passing notes under the table asking, "Check this box if you like me."

Prior to visiting University of Idaho, I had flown to a prestigious college in California. This school also had plenty of alcohol and parties. But unfortunately, at least for them, no lesbians. Well, none that I could find. It was a smaller college, located right outside San Francisco, a.k.a. "Gay World Headquarters". Yes, I know—what on God's green earth was I thinking? Once again, I pictured my exhausted guardian angel trying to help poor, closeted Shaley but I just kept missing the boat.

Driving back to the airport from that California visit, the coach asked me, "So how many more schools are you visiting before you make your decision, Shaley?" Still fatigued from the previous night of drinking I uttered, "Only one more. The University of Idaho," and continued watching the endless stream of palm trees out my window. Then almost as if she was speaking to herself, she said, "I always lose so many girls to Idaho." I tilted my head slightly in confusion, which was met with a punitive throb of pain. A reminder of how much alcohol I'd consumed the previous night. Not wanting to provoke my headache more, I turning slowly back towards the window, catching a glimpse of myself in a side mirror on the way. A boxer who'd clearly lost a fight the night before seemed to be staring back with puffy, bloodshot eyes. So even though her response was intriguing, given my condition, I knew there was zero chance I'd be able to engage in a full-on conversation.

After returning from my University of Idaho experience, however, her comment made perfect sense. As closeted as I was, you could've offered me a full ride to any school in the country and it would've paled in comparison to being surrounded by other lesbians, closeted or not. The heart wants what the heart wants, and my heart was absolutely desperate for love, attention, and the physical touch of a woman.

When I had finished with my college recruitment tours, my father was thrilled that I was seemingly doing so well. He was, I'm sure, also overjoyed at the prospect of someone else paying for my college tuition. He had already paid for two full semesters at the University of Oregon, so I'm certain he was frustrated.

One night, he excitedly asked me to sit down and write out a pro and con list for all the colleges. Basically, going through each school and listing my "likes" and "dislikes." This was so Dad. I sat there with my navy-blue Clark College sweatshirt covering my head, knees bouncing under the table. I could feel his enthusiasm at helping me fine-tune and decide on a school. But let's face it—I already knew the outcome with or without any process of elimination list.

The problem? Convincing Dad. All of the other schools I'd toured had far more to offer in regard to prestige, qualified professors, diverse course selection, and an active campus life. The University of Idaho column *strangely* ended up with all "pros" and only one "con". (Cows). I could see the confusion wash over my dad's face knowing he was thinking, "Why is Idaho dominating so much when there is a plethora of other better choices also being offered?" I kept bullshitting him, making up reasons like, "The campus had a great layout," or, "I really loved the coaches," or, "I just felt like I would really excel there." Inside I was screaming, "Lesbians!"

So, I became an Idaho Vandal. At least it was more intimidating than a penguin or duck. Thoughts of relief filled me, knowing I would finally be around my own kind. Acting like I had my first teenage crush, I giddily bounced around as I packed my bags, readying myself for the long drive with Dad to Moscow. Little did I know, this would be one of the darkest periods of my life. My longtime secret, my constant loneliness, my life of being closeted—they were all merging into the perfect storm.

EIGHT

IDAHO

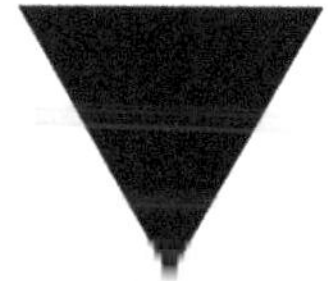

The University of Idaho's mascot was the vandal, a symbol of senseless destruction. Given that I'd been on a senseless self-destructive mission for years, I figured fitting in would be like coming home. As Dad and I made our way through the endless rolling hills of Idaho, my stomach was a flurried concoction of hopeful anticipation and apprehension.

"I'm very proud of you Sha," Dad commented. After a few moments of getting no response he asked, "Did you hear me?"

I blurted, "Yeah…. Yeah, Dad," having no clue what he just said, since I'd been daydreaming out the window, my mind preoccupied, replaying my previous visit to Idaho and being kissed by a woman. Just thinking of when her soft lips touched mine sent a surge of tingles cascading down my spine. As if a switch flipped my body and mind to *alive* mode, impossible to turn off. I craved more. I tried to convince myself I chose Idaho for basketball, but in reality, the university held the one and only thing I desperately wanted—Love. We passed the "Welcome to Moscow Idaho" sign and the warm tingling returned, as if sensing that something extraordinary was on the horizon.

Up till that point, alcohol had been my main go-to. My future painkiller pal, Vicodin, wasn't readily available nor on my radar as another possible escape option. Too bad future me couldn't have beamed down to warn me, "Hey, babe, just letting you know, you might wanna avoid pain pills. Well, and maybe alcohol. Actually, while I'm here, maybe avoid getting that mullet. Not a good look."

I soon discovered at the university, all we fucking did was train, train, train. It was unreal, like I'd signed up for some reality show, "Can You Survive Idaho?" I'd never experienced that degree of continual collegiate-level training.

"What is it with the hyperactive "let's do anything and push our body till we drop' mentality?!" I asked my teammate Christy, as we both gasped for air upon finishing yet another set of sprints. I was crouching with hands on my knees, sweat pouring down, and lungs burning in the September Idaho heat. The acrid smell of cow manure passed over the track and I fought the urge to vomit. "I think they want us in the best shape ever but, yeah, this is a bit overkill," she wheezed in agreement. Tilting my head, I noticed she looked ashen, and her complexion was mottled. "Dude, you don't look good," I said. She smiled faintly back. Then with an audible sigh, we stood up and walked over to start more sprints.

I just didn't understand that sort of physical intensity. I recalled my coaches enthusiastically asking me on my initial visit, "Haven't you ever wanted to run a marathon or do an Iron-man?" I had responded with a matter of fact, "Absolutely not," which was met with awkward, silent stares from everyone. My peanut gallery, and in hindsight my clear "voice of reason," immediately instructed me to leave. *Dude, just leave. Back away slowly and head home.* I was obviously on a different wavelength than my coaches but either ignored it because, well, hello—*LESBIANS*; or I hadn't realized practices would be like training for the *Hunger Games*. My idea of productive training would've been a fun pickup basketball game, then a trip to the bar for beers. You know, team building exercises. Theirs was run five miles, lift weights, play ball, swim three miles, and maybe have a log throwing contest too.

They pushed us to the extreme, wanting us to be in the best athletic condition of our lives which was in a way, admirable. But they were also obsessed with body weight. Yes, body weight. Like wrestlers trying to make their weight class, we had our body fat and weight monitored constantly. It wasn't a shock that many of my teammates developed some level of body dysmorphia. If they didn't have an eating disorder before they came, they sure had one afterward.

As for training, we would start each morning before dawn, lift weights, then after classes, hit the track and run a few miles. Often, we'd end up in the University pool doing water aerobics, water polo, or some other torturous water activity. My mind swirling with confusion, I kept wondering *when* exactly would we play basketball? I was on a *basketball* scholarship, right?

With all the continual hardcore training, not surprisingly, it finally took its toll and something broke. It probably didn't help that I partied and drank all the time, but fuck, even if you weren't a mushrooming alcoholic like me, who wouldn't want a drink to help soothe throbbing muscle aches? I'm sure my body would have fared better without all the alcohol, though. Vicodin was definitely orbiting, as if patiently waiting for the perfect moment to increase the mayhem in my life. The turning point came when I injured my back due to the never-ending team training exercises (or ongoing partying).

The trainers and coaches, I'm certain, thought I was faking. Since nothing showed up on the MRI, I think they assumed I was trying to get out of practice. Honestly, I would have relished the idea of less exercise and skipping practice. But the pain in my back was excruciatingly real. It just wasn't visible. It didn't help matters that sometimes my back felt completely normal. I couldn't figure out what was causing it, as it seemed so random. But when it did strike, it was immediate and felt like someone had stabbed me in my lower back.

After some practices, I'd lumber through my apartment door and become one with the floor. No stopping to remove my stinky, sweat-soaked gear or fix myself dinner. All I wanted to do was lay down and not move a muscle. My lower spine throbbed, radiating waves of needle-like pain down my leg. I'd lay motionless, sometimes for hours, nervous to move even the slightest bit or I'd face the consequence of a bolt of lightning. I'd stare up at my ceiling, wiping the occasional tear from my cheek. I didn't understand what was happening to my body and felt hesitant to ask for more help from the coaches. They'd already taken me to the doctor a few times with no concrete results. I felt like the boy who cried wolf.

Playing sports for so many years, I'd seen my fair share of injuries. But back injuries in particular were fairly complicated to diagnose. And possibly dangerous to treat with that whole spinal cord right in the middle. What doctor wants to mess around with the possibility of accidentally paralyzing someone, particularly someone who isn't even twenty years old? So, unless the ER doctor also happened to an Orthopedic specialist, the best they could do was relieve pain with medication. They'd take out their pad, scribble something barely legible and tell me, "Take 1-2 every four hours for pain." Hello, Vicodin.

As it turned out, I had ruptured one of the lower discs in my back. Yeah, fucking painful. The problem, again, was nothing showed up on any X-rays or MRIs for years. And then there was the intermittent nature of it all. I would be fine for a period of time, then seemingly out of nowhere a piercing pain would hit as I bent over. Often, it happened after I'd been doing nothing but walking across the room then BAM!—a surge of intense fire would stab my lower back and I'd fall to the floor, not daring to move a muscle. "Nobody touch me!" I'd yell repeatedly as tears welled up. Most of the time, I'd end up hobbling into the emergency room, desperate for help. 100% of the time, I'd leave with another prescription.

At that point, I started to question my own reality and sanity. Was I creating all of this drama just to score painkillers? The line was becoming blurred. I knew I was in pain and needed painkillers, but was I subconsciously manifesting the intensity of back pain to score pills? Sort of like the chicken or the egg, both situations led to signals telling my brain I was in pain. But which came first? Years later, when we finally did discover my disc was damaged, I felt strangely vindicated. I knew it wasn't all in my mind. The painkillers did what they were supposed to do. They relieved my pain. The problem was never the efficacy of the pills. The problem, the real problem, was when I crossed the line and actively started seeking them when I wasn't in pain.

Despite the physical exhaustion I endured from practices, I finally got settled. The life I had imagined, of sporty femme lesbians throwing themselves at me, wasn't my reality. In fact, it was the opposite. Sitting in our first team meeting, my stomach full of fluttering butterflies, I saw some of the women from the big lesbian party I met on my recruitment visit. Well, *closeted* lesbian party. I felt my cheeks warm, and a spontaneous smile spread across my face. It was impossible to contain my elation upon seeing them. I had to fight the urge to run over, like a Golden Retriever overjoyed at seeing its owner. A powerful flash of giddy energy rushed through me. But my, let's just call it, "enthusiastic" face, wasn't met with the same fervor. Kathy, who's eyes were normally a welcoming warm brown like *Bambi's*, narrowed into glaring, laser-like darts. Apparently, this golden retriever was in the doghouse, although I had no clue what I'd done wrong.

Catching her rather obvious clue, I stifled my embarrassment and looked down, pretending to be fascinated with the University of Idaho's rules and regulations handout. Kathy proceeded to ignore me and carried on, gleefully greeting other players. Casually leaning on the locker behind me with a "Welcome Shaley" taped to it, I slouched back trying to ignore the poking pain of the locker handle prying into my shoulder. I sat there acting as if I hadn't a care in the world like "Joe Cool" in sunglasses; nothing bothered me. But my body and nerves started telling a different story. A hot heat had already started creeping up my neck, threatening to flush my cheeks a lovely shade of crimson red.

I pretended to be thoroughly absorbed in reading the student conduct rules, hoping no one would notice how obviously phony my acting was and call me out. "Please, for the love of God, just start the fucking meeting!" I desperately pleaded internally, hoping to end my ridiculous theatrical charade. I was trapped. I couldn't leave, was clearly not welcome in certain circles and let's face, there was no chance I'd be having career as a thespian any time soon. Go ahead, you're thinking it. Just say it. "You may not be a *thespian*, but you have a great future as a *lesbian*!" Yes, there's a 12-year-old boy in all of us. Also, if I had to read the one and only sentence I'd been staring at the entire time again, I would've screamed.

Although I'm sure imperceptible to others, I noticed the paper in my hands began to slightly shake. Trying to steady myself, I put the paperwork aside as if I'd fully absorbed all information and was ready to be tested. Then I casually slipped my tremoring hands around the edges of the bench, hoping to miraculously expel my nervous tension into the wood.

A familiar heavy weight settled on my chest. I actually did understand Kathy and the other women's reactions. I knew they were scared and just as deep in the closet. The meeting eventually started, but over the next few weeks, nothing was ever said about all the kissing and flirting that had happened on that first night. Nothing at all. Not even a wink or covert smile from the woman I kissed. It was like I had imagined the entire thing, but I knew I hadn't. It was real. She was real. Yet since I was also deep in my closet of fear, and now embarrassed at my presumption of mutual romance, I joined in, acting like nothing had happened. I convinced myself it was no big deal, and I was being stupid.

Then, once again, I started flirting with boys, pretending I was "normal".

I had an apartment on the edge of campus, away from other students, which made things worse. I felt more alone than I had ever felt before. For starters, I had never lived so far away from all my family and friends. I was hundreds of miles from anything familiar, and my one-bedroom apartment was pretty craptastic. The flimsy walls were a dingy gray, and no matter how many lights I turned on, it remained dark and drafty. Then it started snowing, which one would think would make everything sparkle. I am from Portland, a city that rarely gets a lot of snow, and when it does, everyone loses their shit with kid-like excitement.

Seeing the snow, I ran outside screaming like a toddler on Christmas morning, "It's snowing!" People from Idaho thought there was something wrong with me, while I couldn't figure out what was wrong with them. It was snow! Soon, I understood. It never stopped. It just snowed and snowed, piling up into huge drifts, eventually melting into icky brown slush. Just another appealing selling point of Moscow, Idaho.

I started to hate—yes, hate—all of it. It was cold constantly, and the routine of class, grueling practices, study groups, and trainings were exhausting. Not to mention, my constant longing for women seemed more burdensome than ever. A woman had wanted me, or so I thought. Even if it was only for a brief moment, I had felt what it was like to be attractive to someone, only to have it ripped away. Like kicking someone when they're down, sending me further into a depressing spiral of unworthiness.

The entire experience had brought me to a precipice, pushing me closer to the edge. The pressure to either come out or keep my closet door closed was right outside pounding and demanding a decision. My entire life, I had constantly pretended to be someone I wasn't, which actually did provide a sense of group safety and belonging. Even if I felt like an imposter to that group. But while choosing the "safe" option, I was also denying myself any sort of true, honest love. I wasn't sure how long I could contain my emotions.

One early morning, after a long night of sleeplessness, I sat on the edge of my bed with my elbows on my knees, hands holding my head, just staring down. For a moment, I thought my bathroom faucet was leaking until I realized the light *'tap-tap'* sound I kept hearing was coming from tears hitting the wood floor. There was such a dark, inescapable emptiness inside. I felt like the walking dead, alive and dutifully going through the motions of life, yet inside I was a desolate, vacant, wreck.

Then my survival voice popped up and yelled, "Drinking! What we need is more alcohol!" banishing my emotions. Like the snow that never melted outside my window, I wanted my heart and burning desires to freeze over, - and my fear silenced. The idea that no one cared, and I would never be loved seemed to be constantly lurking in the back of my mind. It's funny the snowballing effect that happens sometimes when you're down. Under the right circumstances, a low level of sadness can easily turn into a tsunami of depression and self-hatred.

Sitting on my kitchen floor with the refrigerator humming at my back, I cracked open a can of Coors light. (I know, ewww) "You're not worthy of love, Shaley, so just give up," kept scrolling like ticker tape at the bottom of my runaway thoughts. Past images of how Mom treated me, especially when Dad was involved, merged with images of the lesbians in Idaho liking me at first, then acting as if I didn't exist.

Each memory shared a common theme. They all looked at me with contempt. I watched as a variety of past scenes played out, each image the same. One minute I'm accepted, the next rejected with their unpredictable stares of judgment. Thinking of the team meeting and how Kathy glared at me, I wrapped my arms even tighter around my knees, as if attempting to squeeze myself out of existence. "Fuck you." I mumbled. "Fuck all of you." Like clockwork, my stomach gurgled, and I sprinted to the bathroom. Even if my truth wasn't coming out that morning, something else did. Wiping my chin, I shakily turned and sat by the toilet, pulling my knees tight once more.

It never dawned on me to tell someone I was gay. Hindsight's always great in realizing problems, big or small, might not be so world-ending if we just came clean. But I had never seen any evidence that it actually would be OK to be an out lesbian. Just the opposite—everywhere I turned, being gay was talked about, openly I might add, as something abnormal and often disgusting. A joke sometimes but an insult all the time. I was embarrassed and feared someone would discover my secret. "Trust me," my dominant inner voice said, "It's much better to live our lie of being straight." Even if inside I was slowly suffocating.

Although drinking helped mask my loneliness, it was becoming increasingly challenging keeping up my front. I felt strange, like there were two of me. One Shaley was vulnerable, scared, and unsure how to behave while the other was bold and fearless, continually showing the world how confident (and of course, straight) she was. I knew inevitably at some point these two "Shaley's" would collide. But the denier and procrastinator in me joined forces continually to make sure that would never happen.

The outer Shaley became more belligerent, numb, and defiant as a result of the alcohol, while the inner one kept trying to manage my almost unbearable pain. Sort of like trying to hold water in a sieve, but in my case, the leaking was anger and resentment. "Why can't I have love? There's nothing wrong with me?" my dejected, internal voice would scream. This was routinely met with my demanding, practical outward voice yelling, "Dude, shut it down! You'll blow our cover!" Like pulling on a thread of a loosely sewn sweater, threatening to unravel everything.

What did I do with all this internal chaos? I got a kitten. She was a little black and white kitten that brightened up my dreary Idaho life. I named her Mittens, because she had adorable little white paws. But I wasn't kidding myself, even then, with why I got her. I was lonely and she gave me unconditional love. There were plenty of people who did love me, the Shaley I presented to the world. I was the life of the party: gregarious, kind, easy to like. "Shaley!" people would shout when I entered a party, like some tall, skinny version of "Norm" from *Cheers*. But it felt like no one actually knew me. How can you truly know someone when a huge part of them is hidden? It's no wonder that in my childhood I coaxed stray animals to come home with me. They were incapable of judgement and, no matter what, always provided love. And they definitely never gave two shits about my sexual orientation.

One afternoon in the locker room, my teammate Melissa asked why I got a kitten. In all fairness to her, it was sort of odd for student athletes to get a pet. I'm guessing she asked purely out of curiosity. Feeling put in the spotlight, I stumbled through my response defensively, "Well, of course because I love animals. And she was cute, so *duh*, why not?" trying to redirect her commentary to imply she was an idiot to even ask. She answered her own question, "I think you're lonely." My heart stopped as my other teammates all paused and looked at me. I brought my towel to my face pretending to wipe away sweat. In reality I needed to momentarily cover my reddening cheeks. I felt naked and exposed. I was used to holding my feelings at bay and up until that moment, I don't think I had consciously realized just how lonely I had become. But she nailed it.

Flushed and trying to swallow my embarrassment, I couldn't make eye contact with anyone so began rummaging around in my locker. If anyone even thought I was lonely, and moreover actually knew it, I would've been mortified. I was supposed to be strong. I didn't need anyone, and I would certainly never open myself up to vulnerability by admitting it. Her words cut through me like a hot knife through butter though. Did she know, or was she guessing?

Funny to be in the juxtaposition of wanting to be seen so desperately, while at the same time praying no one would actually see me. The bigger threat had nothing to do with my adoration of a kitten or even loneliness; I was emotionally filled to capacity and dangerously close to having everything inside spill over. One tiny push was all it would take to break through my floodgate. I felt like I'd been carrying the weight of an invisible elephant on my shoulders and I desperately longed to set it down. Let all secrets out and screw the consequences. But that of course did not happen. Perhaps sensing my embarrassment, she changed the subject before it went further. My moment of crisis averted, we then carried on with whatever gossip was happening that day.

In the end, with my busy schedule and party life, it was too hard to care for Mittens properly, so I gave her to a family in Idaho. That was one of the best decisions, and possibly the only good decision, I made there. Even though animals have some sort of sixth sense, provide continual love, and are usually resilient as all hell, I don't think Mittens would have been up for what was coming. Shit was about to hit the fan. You're welcome, Mittens.

NINE

IT'S TIME TO GO

T he leftover stench of stale beer permeated everything and lingered in the air. It had been another evening of drunken debauchery with my team, and me pathetically chasing Kathy around. Both of us deep in the closet, playing our twisted childlike cat and mouse game. Apparently, she was OK with flirting when a certain level of inebriation had been achieved. When I finally caught up with her outside the hallway bathroom, I charmingly slurred, "Just one little kiss." She leaned in, pretending to kiss me, then ran away laughing, inviting me to continue our game of catch-me-if-you-can. I reluctantly, yet excitedly, took the bait. She was Lucy with the football, while I continued to play Charlie Brown in this never-ending game of rejection.

Around 1:00 a.m., a wall of weariness hit me, leaving me completely drained of energy. My body slumped, as if someone pulled my plug, and I slide awkwardly down the wall with legs sprawled. Alone in the hallway in my drunken stupor, I decided the game we were playing was childish and stupid. But in reality, I just couldn't catch her. Either way it was time to go. "Fine. Be that way!" I shouted at no one and stumbled out into the cold, sloshing my way back to my tiny apartment.

Irritated and fatigued from the evening's roller coaster ride, I tried lifting my spirits by preoccupying my thoughts with food. Well, trying to remember if I actually had food in my fridge. My pace quickened and mouth began to water like some Pavlovian dog as images of warm cinnamon toast filled my thoughts. My sour mood returned quickly, however, when I pulled open my fridge and saw one lone six-pack of beer, half a bottle of ketchup, and some sort of hard molding cheese. Not sure why I thought I'd have the makings for cinnamon toast given I never went shopping but still. "Figures," I moaned as I ripped one of the cans from the plastic ring. My bean bag made a loud *shhooomp* sound, as I fell on top, cracking open the beer with only one hand. I laid there depleted and raw, staring out at the new falling snow.

Waves of emptiness crept in, and soon my thoughts were spiraling deep down the rabbit hole. I felt trapped. I *was* trapped in this hell hole of an apartment, in this cow-stinking town, buried under paralyzing layers of snow. I was trapped in a world where the only solution to living a "normal" life was to pretend to be heterosexual. All I wanted was someone to love me. *Good Lord,* I thought, *If I had a dollar for every time I thought that, I'd, well…have a lot of money,* clearly unable to do simple math in my overly intoxicated state. It seemed like no matter how many creative ways I tried to escape my invisible chains, there would never be a solution where I ended up truly happy. I finished my beer and clumsily threw it across the room, leaving a urine-colored, cloudy Pollock-like masterpiece streaked across my wall.

Grumbling, I grabbed another beer and proceeded to fumble into my bedroom, thinking maybe sleep would help. My mattress was on the floor next to the 1970s lamp I got from my parents. Originally, I was aiming for a sexy bohemian *Starsky and Hutch* slick interior design but ended up with some sort of earth-toned, depressing squatters' den. A couple of abstract cityscape oil paint-ings hung on each wall, also from the '70s. They had been painted with mustard-brown colors, now faded and cracked. Interior de-sign was clearly not my calling.

Topping the whole cozy ambiance off was a 60-watt ceiling light that barely lit the room, leaving most of it hidden in shadows. As I took inventory of my surroundings, I thought, *Well, at least you're consistent with your decorating schemes, Howard.* The entire apart-ment felt dank and musty, and screamed 1970's. Just taking it all in I could almost smell the patchouli/musk incense.

"Ahhhhhhh!" I shouted at the ugly painting. Where did it all go wrong? I was a star player at Clark College. Sure, I partied, but I still managed to get decent grades, graduate, and play fan-tastic basketball. *What the fuck happened to you?* I thought. In Idaho, I was bordering on flunking every class, barely surviving practices and games, and drinking constantly. But something else far more daunting loomed over me. I was sure some of the girls from the team saw me flirting, or trying to flirt, with Kathy.

Sinking into my mattress, a recent conversation between my teammates Sue and Carol flashed through me. "It's just not right," Carol had said. "Just stop," replied Sue, "they're human beings who just happen to be attracted to the same sex." I had been qui-etly walking behind them on pins and needles, unsure of what to do. "Yeah, whatever. I think it's gross," Carol said with obvious contempt. Early on in life, I had learned a great way to stop any uncomfortable conversation was to distract or redirect with other subjects. Sometimes, if the conversation was about "the gays," it was necessary to add my own homophobic commentary to throw the scent off me.

When they noticed me trailing quietly behind, my throat tight-ened. With a forced smile, I blurted, "Well, there's nothing wrong with a little lezzy *licky-licky*." This provoked a round of laughter and provided enough camouflage to stave off any doubts around my heterosexuality.

I mean, what gay person would be making fun of other gays? Oh right, closeted me. Nothing like making disparaging comments about other lesbians, and of course myself, to keep up my front. I looked down, feeling my gut sink with a surge of self-loathing shame. Not wanting the conversation to continue or worse, draw attention to my flushing cheeks, I immediately changed the topic, "Hey, do you know who's starting in tomorrow's game?"

As I laid there thinking of that interaction, tears welled up in my eyes. I had overheard similar homophobic conversations, or been part of them, all my life. Each one chipped away a small piece of me, over and over. Each homophobic slur. Each disgusting look. Every snide comment. Every gay joke. I heard them all, even when people thought they were whispering. The rare person who had the courage to defend gays or stand up to such bigotry, still always seemed to refer to us as, "those people". We were always outsiders.

Staring up at my solitary lightbulb, I let out a deep, guttural groan. The weight of everything seemed to be pressing down and a level of fatigue I'd never experienced enveloped me. It wasn't like the extreme fatigue I was so familiar with after a hard practice, or even a long night of partying. My legs and body felt almost paralyzed as if lead was sluggishly pulsing through me instead of blood. I laid there with blurry eyes feeling almost catatonic. Even the smallest movement seemed impossible. Well except lifting the can of beer to my mouth.

I couldn't seem to interrupt the repetitive negative messages my mind kept spinning about homosexuals being subhuman abominations. And underneath the destructive looping rhetoric was my heavy heart, deeply lonely. No matter how hard I tried to strategize a way out, I kept hitting a dead-end. I couldn't take it anymore.

The light stream of tears that had started moments before increased and began to soak my pillowcase like an oblong watermark slowly expanding. Drunk, angry, and inconsolable, I began to sob deeply. My body, already trembling, soon started to convulse as I began spewing out a string of incoherent words. My two Shaley personas were trying to exist in a world where only one would be accepted. Like Mad Max of Thunder-dome, "Two people enter, one person leaves!" *Who will be the winner?*

One Shaley was a tough, sarcastic, heterosexual-wannabe and the other a scared, tender, insecure homosexual. Another epic battle for control was playing out in my remote solitude. The struggle between the inner and outer me was searching for a way to coexist or die; I felt like a gay Jekyll and Hyde. The problem, of course, is that they were both me, and each version of me seemed to be causing copious amounts of damage. One was destroying my body and mind with drugs and alcohol, while the other believed she wasn't worthy of love, and lived in denial, pretending to be someone she wasn't. I'm not sure which was more damaging. All of me felt like I was slowly fading away though, or wanted to.

My guttural cries grew louder as I spewed out a nonsensical, garbled monologue. "*Why?* Why am I here? No one loves me. No one cares! Mom *sure* didn't love me…why me? What the fuck did I do to deserve this?" This internal and external wailing continued as I faded in and out of consciousness. At one point, I woke up with my head throbbing. Staring at the ceiling, teardrops began to pool, the salt stinging my already bloodshot eyes. The constant dull, heavy ache in my heart felt inescapable as I put both hands on my chest, attempting to sooth and console myself. Repeatedly, I began to pray for a small ounce of relief and for someone, or something, to spare me this agony.

Maybe they were right? I thought. *Maybe I'm not worthy of love.* I wanted to die. It hadn't been the first time this thought had crossed my mind, but in my drunken state and feeling like everything had come to a head, this time I really wanted out. To simply not exist anymore. With blurry eyes and snot now mixing with my tears, the chaotic sobbing started again. I didn't care about anything anymore. There was no point—I was looking right into my own abyss and all I saw was an ocean of emptiness. A lifetime of pretending and loneliness. With eyes puffy and weary heart, I mumbled a resigned, "No one is coming, Shaley."

Clearly having a meltdown, I thought, "Why not call my sister Laurie?" She was the only person who always got me. All the shit we had to deal with growing up, all the times we watched Mom use us, or yell, or fall apart—through it all we had each other. She was the only person, besides our dad, who was always there. I picked up the phone and dialed. No answer. I dialed again, trying to regain some semblance of mental control and stability, while hiccupping my sobs back, waiting for her to pick up. *Ring….* Silence. *Ring….* Silence.

It was now around 3:00 a.m. I was trying to maintain my composure when her answering machine picked up with, "Hi! You've reached the Wilson's. Leave a message at the tone, and we'll get back to you as soon as possible." Hearing her voice on the machine, I instantly fell apart. My voice cracked as I shakily said, "Laurie, are you there?" Nothing. I proceeded to leave her another seven or eight, let's just say, unfortunate messages, detailing my current state of mind. *Good morning and you're welcome*, I thought later. Not good. Each time, I sobbed a series of incomprehensible messages through the phone, not at all considering how much they would freak her out. It was not my finest moment.

But by that point I was incapable of thinking about anyone else. And I didn't care. I was so angry and hurt, drowning in a deep, self-absorbed victim mindset, it was impossible to think of anyone but myself. Was I supposed to live this awful life to keep other people happy? I mean, for fuck's sake, I had been in some sort of limbo and pain since childhood, and it never got better. And right then, it was *by far* the worst I'd ever felt.

There was a psychology experiment done back in the 1960s using dogs. It was an experiment on classical conditioning and "learned helplessness". In this experiment, the subject, in this case dogs, were put in a shock box. There were three groups, and each had to endure repeated electric shocks, or "aversive stimuli." Each group of dogs was given a different level of control to stop the electric shocks. But in the last group, there was no way to stop the shocks. Realizing there was no way out and they had no control, the last group of subject dogs eventually stopped trying to escape or fight back. They just laid there, helpless.

When I had first learned of that experiment, I was stunned that any human would be so cruel to test this on dogs. The outcome of the experiment, however, never left me. I felt like that caged animal, desperately looking for an escape. And even though I wasn't receiving electric shocks, my pain was excruciatingly real. I had searched for an answer for years but like those poor dogs, it felt like there was no way out. It was time to let go of these false identities, stop fighting, and just lay down.

The next few minutes felt surreal, as if I was an outsider watching myself on a movie screen. In slow motion, I stood up and staggered into the bathroom. Sliding the vinyl shower curtain aside, I leaned in and picked up my plastic Daisy razor. My face contorted momentarily as I stood back up, feeling a pierce of pain hit my temples. My skull felt as if it was being crushed in a vice. But as quick as the pounding pain hit me, it faded. Almost as if it was dismissed and no longer registered as important. Some sort of primal mindset took over, numbing all pain and leaving me vacant of critical thinking. There were no more tears, no more guttural cries. I was like an overloaded circuit breaker that had finally tripped—an empty, emotionless vessel proceeding on autopilot.

I woke with swollen eyes and a parched cotton mouth. "Some party," I moaned pushing down a wave of nauseousness. Then everything that had happened rushed back. I frantically looked down at my wrist and saw what I had done. The sheets where my arm had been laying were stained in a small, rippled pink circle. The room spun as I sprinted to the bathroom. Rinsing my arm and wrist to see the damage, and seeing no deep tissue wounds, the tension in my body momentarily relaxed. Then my stomach lurched, and I whirled around just in time to vomit into the toilet. I stayed there hugging the cool porcelain letting it ease my furious pain. My head was a constant barrage of confusion and noise as a stream of rather unfortunate memories of the previous night unfolded. As if on cue, my peanut gallery chimed in laughing at my rudimentary suicide skills, "*Dude, even your attempt to escape your fucked-up life was fucked.*" It was good to know even in my darkest times, at least I had the company of that sarcastic crew.

It was right about then that I remembered my messages to Laurie. *Well, shit. The cat's out of the bag now, Shaley.* It's funny, you'd think that after having an atomic meltdown on Laurie's answering machine, that would've been the perfect time to come out. I mean, I was already pretty fucking low so why not just let it all out? But no. I was still terrified to admit I was gay. So, I decided to go with the very reasonable explanation of how much I hated Idaho and felt completely lost. I mean I *was* completely lost and confused, but that certainly wasn't the impetus for trying to step off the edge. There I was, still drowning in an ocean of pain and despair from being closeted, creating more lies to cover it all up.

Underneath the strategizing supersonic brain that continually managed my survival, there was a heavy melancholy that never left. At what point would I be able to simply let go and be free? I felt like I was thrown into this insane world where my survivor instinct was constantly activated. Ultimately, I just wanted to escape my pain, not my actual life. But what felt like very real terror of someone discovering I was gay consumed me. Everything else in my life might have been hard, possibly depressing, but nothing I was going through would have sent me to that suicidal edge. That was from years of feeling unworthy and being denied love. Plain and simple.

Laurie and Dad, of course, freaked. Laurie expressed herself by sobbing into the phone. Dad spoke calmly, but I could hear the fear and falter in his voice. He said he was coming to get me. All I could do was cry. I felt like a child. Hell, in that moment I *was* a child, needing other people to take care me. My life was clearly falling apart. There I was, a grown ass adult woman, living in a shithole apartment in the middle of nowhere and flunking out of the college that had eagerly recruited me. I had an escalating substance abuse problem and was barely able to get out of bed. I couldn't seem to do anything right, let alone live authentically. Hell, I couldn't even figure out how to attempt suicide right. Although, perhaps not excelling at that was a good thing.

Later that morning, I heard an assertive, soft knock on my door. It was my assistant coach, Sherrie. I am almost certain both of my coaches were gay. I have no idea if they were out to anyone, but they definitely weren't out to me. It certainly would've helped my situation if someone who *was* gay, even a closeted gay, had stepped in to assure me that I wasn't an abnormal freak, alone in my misery. But it was a different time, in a little town in Idaho in the late 1980s. My guess is, if they had been out of the closet, at a bare minimum, they would have been major targets for harassment. And they could've kissed their coaching careers goodbye.

"Hey," I mumbled, as I unlocked my door. "Hey there," she replied in a gentle, concerned voice. I motioned her in, and she hugged me immediately, "I'm so glad you're OK." I leaned into her embrace, aching for more but self-conscious of my disheveled appearance and rank odor. I stood there cringing with swollen red eyes and unkempt hair, wearing the only long sleeve shirt I could find to cover my arms. She proceeded to ask me a few probing questions trying to fully absorb the gravity of the situation. Yet with all her questioning, the one elephant-in-the-room question of, "Are you gay?" that should've been asked, was never brought up by either of us.

Resting casually against the door frame with crimson cheeks, I could hardly make eye contact. Even though I had spiraled into chaos the previous night, there I was, still trying to act nonchalant. "What's that? Oh no, I'm fine. Why do you ask? This isn't just a friendly 8a.m. Sunday visit?"

When she asked to look at my wrists, I had to fight the mounting tears already stinging the back of my eyes, threatening to pour out. I was so ashamed. All I could do was look down at my peeling kitchen floor. I pulled up my shirt sleeve and held out my arm while she gingerly removed the bandages I'd haphazardly wrapped around. Fortunately, what I'd done to myself didn't warrant a visit to the hospital. A psychiatric facility, perhaps, but not the hospital. And hell, maybe that's where I belonged. "Finally—a place where I would fit in!" I mumbled with a chuckle. I could see the wheels in her brain trying to comprehend why I was grinning in such a serious moment, but instead of asking, she just reached out for another hug.

Not surprisingly I ended up leaving Idaho. Leaving under those circumstances was absolutely heart wrenching. I had been this big deal player and felt I'd let everyone down. My Dad, the players, my coaches and ultimately, myself. I don't know what the coaches told everyone, but I could almost see the eyerolls from some people when I offered up my lame boiler-plate reason of "I hate Idaho." Most were kind though; I'm sure sensing it ran much deeper. I mean, nobody suddenly leaves in the middle of a term unless something urgent happened. And even though I could sense their compassion, when they couldn't look me in the eye, I also felt their pity. There were a few who vented their opinions rather loudly. It hurt, but I understood and just took it. They didn't understand. How could they? I was lying about who I was, and then instead of coming clean, I added more lies to my ever-growing mountain of lies. "Fuck, Howard, you are just a constant train of lies, aren't you?" I told myself. Then wondered at what point does a person starts to believe their own lies?

Despite my suicide attempt, I actually loved and appreciated life often. Yes, I'm aware that sounds a bit twisted and fucked up. But there were countless things that filled me with joy. Like the fresh smell of spring rain or a warm summer breeze. Or a long, hard bellyache from a hearty laugh. Or the elation I felt after a long run. I hadn't ever stopped appreciating life's richness. It was the weight of my loneliness and contemplating a life without love that I couldn't, or didn't, know how to handle.

My head rested against the window as Dad drove us through the curved roads back to Portland. A strange melancholy filled me as I numbly gazed out the window. Everything we passed seemed to glow with beauty. Never-ending rolling hills of pale-yellow wheat painted against the cobalt-blue, winter sky was visually stunning. Yet contrasting my beautiful external view was a level of internal shame and depression I had never experienced so deeply. I wasn't sure if, or even how, I'd survive what I'd done. Or what the future held. But underneath all the confusion and pain, I knew there was a fighter, and she was still there. Wounded and scarred, but still alive.

When we finally crossed the border from Idaho to Oregon, I never once looked back. What would've been the point? I had learned what I needed from Idaho.

TEN

I'M HERE AND DEFINITELY QUEER

As predicted, I was handled with kid gloves when I returned home. I knew why I was suffering and such a mess, but they didn't. And I understood the reason for concern. No one knew for certain I wouldn't contemplate death by suicide again. I also knew that what I'd just put everyone through was outrageous and incredibly self-centered. When you're spiraling down the rabbit hole, however, other people's feelings are rarely a consideration—but I hadn't completely lost touch with reality and how my actions affected others. The underlying guilt I felt never abated and definitely took its toll on my poor stomach which felt queasy almost daily.

The entire experience seemed surreal. I found myself wondering, *Did I really do all that insane shit?* Then I'd look down at the scarring on my wrist, as if needing confirmation. I couldn't help feeling like my entire life had been one continuous toilet flush. No matter how hard I tried to escape, solid ground eluded me; I was constantly floating in and out of limbo. All I kept thinking was that the "Idaho ordeal" would remain with me until the cows came home, which brought on a quiet laugh. At least I still had my sense of humor. I would not miss Idaho—or those cows.

After spending years living on my own, moving back in with Dad and Geri was my personal hell. I say that with love. I went from the frying pan into the fire. OK, perhaps it wasn't *that* melodramatic. But when you've been on your own for years, returning to living with parents is challenging. Suddenly, I was thrust into the role of child again. We all have those roles we so easily slide into unconsciously: parent-child, teacher-student, boss-employee. We can't help it.

For outsiders, I'm sure my behavior looked childlike. Poor little Shaley. I partied and flunked out of college, my drinking was out of control, and Daddy had to pick me up and carry me home. I wasn't exactly the posterchild for "adulting." But still, I felt like I traded one nightmare for another. My mouth dropped when Dad said, "Honey, we need you home by ten p.m." Yep, they literally gave me a curfew.

It took less than a year before I realized not only did I want to escape my parents' house, I also desperately wanted to return to university. Even with all the partying I did at Clark College, I was proud I'd still received my associate's degree. But now I was shooting for that four-year one. When I shared my plan with Dad, his face instantly lit up with joy. And relief. Both he and Geri probably wanted me out of their house just as much as I wanted to leave. "I've been hoping you'd tell me that, Sha," he blurted out, wrapping me in a warm bear hug.

Next thing I knew, I was on yet another road trip with Dad, heading south towards the University of Oregon. "This time," I informed him sitting straight up in the passenger seat, "I'm gonna get good grades, Dad." And I thoroughly believed that to my core. He was footing the bill for everything, as no more basketball scholarships were on the horizon. "I signed up for the quiet dorm," I continued as we drove, "It's close to my classes and they don't allow parties." *What? A commitment to get better grades and no partying?* My overly sardonic peanut gallery chimed. Ignoring them, I watched my dad as he continued to nod in acknowledgment while staring ahead, methodically watching traffic merge. Even though he remained semi-stoic, I could see a slightly suppressed grin from the side, exposing his hidden delight.

I did end up getting outstanding grades, almost straight A's—the first term. Then I met Amy who just happened to be in the dorm room at the end of my hall. She was this scrawny, sarcastic Southerner with big opinions and a presence that made me blush. She was perfect. Both of us being closeted, however, made things a little challenging. Not knowing how to communicate that I was head-over-heels, I resorted to the *uh-so successful* adolescent flirtatious behavior I'd perfected in Idaho. I found myself trying to woo her by following her around and insulting her.

"What on Earth is this crap?" I demanded as I made myself at home, sitting cross-legged in the middle of her dorm room bed. "Nothing Compares 2 U, by Sinéad O'Connor," she calmly replied, handing me the CD case. I looked down at an image of a woman with piercing blue eyes and a shaved head, trying to hide my astonishment. Immediately my heart started racing. I'd never known any women with shaved heads, let alone ones that looked like, well, beautiful lesbians. A woman with a shaved head? She must be gay. Duh.

The tiny dorm room suddenly felt smaller and 10 degrees warmer as my face began to burn. Staying true to my adolescent form, when feeling uncomfortable I proceeded to get louder, more disrespectful, and insufferable. "Ugh what's wrong with her? Why doesn't she have *hair*?" I snapped, in a desperate and I'm sure obvious, attempt to hide my embarrassment. Ignoring my snide comment, she casually replied, "I think she's hot." Hearing that my body froze, as if any movement might threaten to expose my crushing vulnerability. Every hair on my neck stood straight up and a thin sheen of sweat broke out all over, like I was a 50-year-old perimenopausal woman.

Cue my immediate exit. I rushed out, hearing the Sinead O'Connor CD clunk on the floor and Amy saying something inaudible. I think it was, "Um, OK, see you later?" I couldn't hear a thing over the blood pounding in my eardrums. When all else fails, run away. Amy was probably so confused as I was always bursting in without an invitation, informing her that her music and dorm decorations sucked, then abruptly departing. Of course, what she didn't know was each time after my bombardment of insults, I'd run away internally screaming, "I love you!"

Even back in Idaho, with all my running around intoxicated on alcohol and hormones, my attempts at "flirting" were never out in the open. In fact, not once in my life was I afforded the opportunity to practice the awkward teenage dance of flirting. I had serious arrested development in the art of romance—not fair. Straight kids had opportunities to attempt the cringe-worthy, prepubescent wooing of their crushes. When you're young and foolish, you're allowed a grace period to fall on your face. As an adult, though, I was clearly a bit stunted in my wooing abilities.

My unsophisticated and juvenile interactions with Amy went on for a while. Strangely, she allowed me to continue with my exasperating badgering as I followed her around like a deranged lost puppy. In hindsight? Duh, of course she did. I may have been a bumbling, obnoxious jerk, but I'm sure on some level she also realized I liked her. But I was scared to death of dropping my tough sarcastic façade, though, and confess my true feelings. Certain if I did, she would recoil with disgust and my life would be over.

Then it happened. One night, we were watching *Fried Green Tomatoes*, a favorite lesbian movie of the 1990s. We had both scrunched up next to each other on my rather uncomfortable twin bed, and then, we *kissed!* Amy had simply rolled over and kissed me! I was shocked. Then, with my face beaming bright red, first from ecstasy followed quickly by trepidation, I realized I had absolutely no idea what to do. Obviously, I had not been given a "Birds and the Bees: Lesbian Edition" talk. But there was no way in hell I was going to stop.

After years of watching everyone around me find love and experience the euphoria of someone you're aching for desire you, it was finally happening to me. This gorgeous woman was kissing me! I kept thinking, *She wants me! Holy fuck! She wants me!* I might have actually been saying that out loud, I'm not really sure. I was fairly blissed-out.

At some point I chuckled quietly through a grin plastering my face. "What?" she asked noticing the weird, abrupt interruption to our kissing. Nervous to share I shyly said, "I just thought of my first crush, Mrs. Aguirre. I always wrote 'A+S' heart doodles on my Pee-Chee's when she was my teacher. Your name is Amy so," I paused, "there's the 'A'." Her smile at that implication made my heart melt, and she began to softly kiss me again. Yes, after a lifetime of my love and desires always being one-sided, someone *else* was finally drawing "A + S" heart doodles.

The thing about finding that someone who loves you is it gives you courage. Or perhaps they simply help you see the courage you already possessed. Amy certainly made me feel more confident than I'd ever felt before—in a multitude of ways. We did everything together. She was my soulmate. At least I thought so at the time. Come on, she was my first love, what can you do? Everyone thinks the first person they fall in love with will be their lifelong partner. You can't imagine your life without them.

It's funny how ignorance dominates so much of our lives. Until it doesn't. I think it would be incredible to go back in time with the more practiced, mature, and wise mindset we have as adults. Just think of all the ridiculous things we do, say, and believe until we have more knowledge and experience. Then we realize we are all so unbelievably young and naive. It's laughable to think that the very first person you're with will end up being your lifelong partner. Some people do find that, but most do not. It's silly. Falling in love for the first time, we believe 100% that there is no way that love won't last forever. That's how I felt with Amy.

We spent the rest of the school year navigating a dorm life that was void of almost any privacy. Fortunately, I had a dorm room all to myself so Amy would sneak down when no one else was in the hallway, knock softly, and I'd let her in. After spending two terms having to hide our blossoming, secret relationship, though, we decided it was time to move out. When Spring term ended, we moved in together. I mean, just because we were closeted lesbians didn't mean we wouldn't still be the stereotypical, "I know we just met but let's immediately live together," also known as, "U-Haul lesbians."

We had come out to a small, select group of other lesbians in the Eugene community, but overall, no one else knew we were gay. Or a couple. But we still proceeded to move into a tiny, one-bedroom apartment just off campus. As we signed the apartment lease I cynically thought, "Let's see how this plays out sunshine. I'm sure *no one* will notice anything odd about two women sharing a microscopic, one-bedroom apartment."

The apartment itself was filled with massive, bulky Fred Flintstone-like furniture literally attached to the floor. Neither of us could understand who would want to steal the ugly couches but we simply arranged our belongings around the permanent fixtures. The kitchen had ancient appliances, the walls were paper-thin, and the bathroom had a toilet that never seemed to stop running. But rent was only $150 a month, so yeah, it was worth it.

Even though the eyesore of an apartment was completely dilapidated, we were so caught up in loving each other that nothing else mattered. I mean we were in Love with a capital "L"! Our closet doors had been flung wide open (at least to each other) and we reveled in our rose-colored, "I love you to the end of time" glasses. The heavenly highs of finding love and experiencing a freedom I'd never had before was unfortunately also mixed with gut-wrenching anxiety. It was hard to feel completely elated when I had one foot still firmly rooted inside my closet.

That summer, my sister Laurie, who also lived in Eugene, managed to get me a dishwashing job at the restaurant where she worked. I was grateful for the extra cash but let's face it, dish washing is the worst. The bright side was I got to see Laurie often. One morning after the breakfast rush, she came back where I was working to chat. Nothing special, just catching up on the latest family gossip. I loaded plates into the bulky commercial dishwasher as we babbled back and forth—a stream of typical sister talk. Then seemingly out of nowhere, Laurie casually inserted, "Is Amy gay?" abruptly ending our fun flowing conversation.

I immediately flinched at the inquiry and watched in slow motion as the dish I was holding slipped from my hands. Luckily, I was standing on an industrial strength rubber mat, so it didn't shatter, which would've drawn even more unwanted attention to a now seriously uncomfortable conversation. Bending over to pick up the plate, I turned my head so she couldn't see how quickly it paled to the color of an anemic ghost. With my back to her pretending to work, I tried regaining my composure scrambling for some sort of plausible, yet nonchalant response. Then, slick as sludge, I stuttered, "Well…no. Don't…don't be ridiculous." She glanced up from her coffee and said, "Oh well, you're together constantly and live in a fairly small, one-bedroom apartment, so I was just wondering."

Oh, she knew. She totally knew. "No," I continued, "We switch days for who gets to sleep in the bed." Dumbest answer ever. Even as it came out of my mouth, my peanut gallery was on the floor laughing. Samuel L. Jackson, who'd been a voice in my gallery for years, was crying hysterically, "Right. You both take *turns* sleeping on the bed and that hard-ass Fred Flintstone couch. *Right.*"

Laurie, being Laurie, let it go. She was like that. Intuitive and smart yet loving and kind. She knew I was gay; she was just testing the waters. I suppose it was easier to ask if Amy was gay than ask if I was. Remaining in the closet was becoming increasingly unbearable. Each day, the weight of my lies seemed to grow exponentially. "Tick tock, motherfucker," Samuel L. Jackson kept saying, always happy to point out the obvious. It was one thing to be closeted and fantasize about being with a woman when I was alone. It was a whole new ballgame actually *being* with a woman. My pretending was nearing an end.

Amy and I made the decision to come out at the same time. We figured if shit hit the fan, we'd at least have each other. Our decision finalized, the heavy reality of what we were doing began to sink in. I'd had a lifetime of pretending, feeling like an imposter in my own life. Unable to sleep after our decision, I stared up vacantly, running through various coming-out scenarios while simultaneously wondering if my apartment's popcorn ceiling contained asbestos. My thoughts ping-ponged restlessly back and forth, "Will my family really be OK with this?" to, "What does asbestos poisoning look like?" then, "How will my friends—especially those who've known me for years—react?" back to, "Asbestos, really? Why put a deadly poison in a product where people live?" No answer to any of these (nor much sleep) came that night.

Amy's family happened to be visiting the Oregon coast that summer, so it was the perfect time for her to tell everyone at once. On the other hand, since my mom and dad were no longer together, I had the joy of *two* coming out parties ahead of me. Although nothing about coming out at the time seemed like it would be a party. If you counted my four sisters who all lived in different places, in actuality I had about six coming out "parties" I dreaded.

Out of my entire family, it was the idea of coming out to my dad that intimidated me the most. I loved him so much—almost idolized him. I had always put him on a pedestal, unable to see his imperfections. So, instead of calling or asking if we could meet, I took the chickenshit way out and mailed him a letter. This was before email existed so snail mail it was, which was fine by me. "The longer it takes, the better. Right, Procrastination Patty?" I thought laughing to myself referring to the obvious lesbian *Peanuts* character Peppermint Patty. I then took off to go camping for a week with Amy and a few other new lesbian friends, trying to delay any possible condemnation or rejection. I knew I wouldn't be able to bear it.

You'd think having grown up with a large family of progressive, highly educated, liberal Unitarians, I wouldn't have been so nervous. The world around me was still abundant with homophobic assholes, but when it came to social justice, my family had never wavered in their tolerance and love. It was the 1990s, the "Don't ask, don't tell" era. I suppose it was society's baby step towards gay and lesbian acceptance, "OK, we know you're probably there serving, just please just don't tell us!" The funny thing is, if there is one group of people I'd never mess with, it would be a bunch of badass, armed, butch lesbians. "Don't ask, don't tell" was very shortsighted of the military in my opinion.

As for telling my mom, it was just happenstance that she called me a few days after Amy and I had made our decision. I was sitting down with a fresh bowl of ramen when the phone rang. "Hi, Mom," I answered. "Oh, *hi*, honey!" she replied in her cheerful phone voice. She immediately started in on, well, anything and everything. To say Mom was loquacious would've been an understatement. She was definitely blessed with the gift of gab.

I listened feeling my heart rate rapidly increase, knowing at some point in this conversation I would tell her. *Just do it, Shaley!* I kept pushing. Ironically, she was carrying on about how the next time we were in town, we should all go to Darcelle XV, which was a hilarious, famous drag show in Portland. I kept patiently listening, sitting on the edge of the Flintstone couch, staring at my now-cold noodles. A light layer of sweat was already coating my face and hands. So much so, at one point I had to use my napkin to wipe down the phone.

I kept trying to get a word in, "Mom. Mom…. I have some…." This went on for a few minutes. Finally, realizing I would never be able to get a word in unless I interrupted, I blurted, "Mom, I'm gay!" You'd think at that point there might a pause or a sliver of acknowledgment. But we're talking about my mom. She just kept going on about plans. With a more forceful tone I interrupted again, "Did you hear what I said, Mom? I'm gay." After almost a full minute of heart stopping silence she said softly, "Yes, honey, I heard you. I just want you to always remember I love you. And to never, no matter what, waste your time on ignorant people."

Tears streamed down my face as I felt my heart fill with love. For all the crazy unbelievable things she put me through, in that moment, she was my mom and she loved me no matter what. Relief flooded me as if I was shedding years of grief, the weight of a heavy winter coat, no longer needed, falling to the floor. Then, as my body felt like it was going through some sort of energizing metamorphosis, she continued her monologue, as if nothing happened.

As for my father, I returned from my camping trip only to be greeted by the red-light blinking of our answering machine. Like a distress signal, it was pulsating on then off, on then off. Warning me. I knew it was from him. Within seconds, my entire nervous system switched from peaceful calm to nail-biting trepidation. "Play it," Amy said without hesitation. "Yeah, easy for you to say, it's not your father," I replied. She knew how scared I was at the thought of his rejection. I could feel the acid in my gut rising as I pressed play. "You have one new message," the automated voice said. "Hi, Sha, it's Dad. I got your letter. I just, well…I feel like my world is crumbling," he said in a somber, crackling voice.

The rest of his message faded into background noise as I sat there in disbelief, dumbfounded. Amy immediately seeing my distress, walked over and gave me a big hug. I couldn't believe it. *His* world was crumbling? What about mine? I was outraged and on the verge of a breakdown. *Does Dad really not approve? The person I thought knew me so well. The one person who'd always been there for me.*

I picked up the phone and dialed. He answered right away. "Hey, Dad, I got your message," I snapped. I'm not sure if I was trying to be confrontational or if I just needed to have the first word. "Hi Sha. Hon, I got your letter. I want you to know I'm not upset, and I love you." I proceeded to ask him what he meant by "his" world was crumbling. His answer was that it took him by surprise and felt personal. "Your daughter being gay is somehow a personal affront to you?" I said incredulously. "And how could it be a surprise?"

Denial is an interesting beast. Geri would tell me years later that my family actually sat him down, prior to me coming out, and told him, "Chuck, we think Shaley might be gay." To which he said, "No, that's not possible." Yes, denial is one ugly monster that we think saves us from pain, but ultimately it does nothing but add to it. We can be so close to something or someone we love yet blinded by our own selfishness or fear that we're unable to see the obvious. In this case, his daughter, the big lesbian right in front of him.

I loved him so deeply, I found myself wanting to step into denial myself, and excuse his reaction away. It would've been easier to simply gloss over the unpleasantness and difficulty of it all. I wanted to play it down as if it wasn't a big deal. But it was a big deal. I understood *why* he was hurting, but of all the people I needed support from, I needed him most. He knew every single crappy thing that I'd been through. He saw my pain, often firsthand, and seriously? *How on earth could you miss I was a big lesbian, Dad?"*

We talked for a while, and he continued to reassure me of his unconditional love. I felt like Humpty Dumpty, dangerously close to a fall in my desperate need for his acceptance. To say I wasn't disappointed by my dad's initial reaction would be dishonest. *I* was the person who'd been closeted and denied romantic love all my life. I had to walk through a judgmental, homophobic world where the majority of people assumed being gay was abnormal and wrong. He didn't have to pretend not to notice people staring like he was some disgusting freak of nature. The least he could have done was ratchet down his selfish parts and share any disappointments or fears he had with Geri, not his daughter. But I was able—eventually—to let his original 'unenthusiastic' response go. Well…*after* I shared all those thoughts with him, I let it go.

I think some parents spiral into a self-absorbed hole when they realize their child is gay. I actually understood my dad's initial reaction. His daughter was living in a world that hated gay people. He wasn't stupid, he knew the world was pretty fucking homophobic. He was also used to feeling in control, so I'm sure the feeling of helplessness was a slight to his senses. There wasn't a whole lot he could do to make life easier for me, accept assure me at least I had his love.

He knew most people wouldn't take the time to get to know me as a person. They'd take one look at me as an out, more masculine looking lesbian and pass judgment. Many would call me awful names, perhaps even threaten me, simply because I was gay. Oddly enough, I knew his initial reaction came from a place of deep love and ultimately, the pain of being unable to protect me. So, he unconsciously (and egotistically) made it about himself. At some point, he realized he wasn't the person who had to deal with the bigotry head on, every single day. Trust me, living life as a gay or lesbian person and directly feeling the brutality of homophobia is much harder than being a bystander.

Coming out to my sisters was rather uneventful. None of them seemed to care, and it certainly didn't change the way they thought about me in the least. My sister Beth, who was perhaps the most laid-back sister out of all of us, casually said, "You know,

I often wondered why more women aren't attracted to each other. I mean, it just seems like women connect better. And I've always known it's not a choice. If it was, I would've chosen women a long time ago." This made me chuckle. Then my heart swelled with love, and I had to blink back the tears starting to form in the corners of my eyes. It was said with such deep contemplation and humor but also undeniable acceptance.

All of my sisters, I'm certain, were a bit relieved when I finally finished coming out to everyone. Most likely, they all had known for years I was batting for the same team and were tired of tiptoeing around it. When I told Larisa, she, well, just started bawling. She kept hugging me and repeating "I love you," over and over, crying tears of joy. There were so many tears and hugging at one point I started to laugh. "OK. I get it. You love me and don't care. I love you too."

When I had my talk with Laurie, she also immediately hugged me, then said, "Fucking *finally!*" There was a moment of silence after her comment, then we both fell apart laughing. We couldn't stop. It was a cathartic laughter that seemed to wash away all the pain. At least momentarily. We laughed. Then we cried. Then we laughed some more. Both of us reaching for the Kleenex I said, "I feel like we should be on some sappy afternoon special right now like '*Sappho and Her Sisters*,' which only increased our laughter.

My Dad eventually redeemed himself for his original comments and, in fact, went to the pro-gay extreme, becoming a leading member of our community PFLAG and an outspoken voice for gay and lesbian equality. There was no LGBTQIA+ then, just gays and lesbians being recognized. But there is no doubt in my mind, if the more inclusive rainbow alphabet soup existed then, he still would have been out, fighting for *everyone's* rights.

With his methodical, type-A personality, Dad often made all of us laugh. "Oh no, here come *Spock*," one of us would say after asking why the sky was blue. He'd proceed to explain scientifically exactly why the sky was blue. I think in many ways, it made sense to him. If there was a problem, you study every aspect of it, then by the process of scientific deductive reasoning, search for a plausible solution. It was just logical to view life through that sort of lens.

What amazed me was as a cis-gender, white, straight, and very privileged man, he took it upon himself to learn everything he could about being gay in this culture. Many people don't take that on, even if someone close to them is gay. After his "my world is crumbling" meltdown, he snapped out of it and started to research the hell out of anything and everything queer.

At times it was challenging of course, because being a lesbian wasn't a mathematical problem to solve. But behind his continual barrage of questions, I knew he wanted to understand. He wanted to show me his love.

Shortly after I came out, any catching up we did was primarily over the phone as he was a dean at Western Michigan University, and I was still in Eugene. Each time we'd talk, he'd make comments like, "Well, the *homosexuals* are making progress in the state of…" And every time I'd roll my eyes and laugh, explaining, "Dad, really. You can say gay or lesbian. You don't have to be so formal calling us homosexuals. It's a little weird." I understood though, and thoroughly appreciated his efforts. He didn't mean to offend me or us "homosexuals." It was the way his mind worked. He got there eventually. We both did.

One week we were catching up and he shared that he'd attended a brown bag lunch with a group of "homosexuals" the previous Wednesday. Then he corrected himself and said, "Lesbians." "What?!" I said in surprise, "Why were you eating lunch with lesbians?" "I thought I'd reach out and get to know them of course." As if this was normal behavior. He meant well, even if it all seemed like one of his science experiments.

Knowing my dad, I'm certain he went to the lunch wanting to understand the world of homosexuals, like we were some alien visitors and spoke a foreign language only we could decipher. God love him. It was a combination of his eager desire for scientific data and his need for a more complete and thorough understanding of gay culture—all motivated by love.

"Dad, here's the thing," I said, "I really appreciate you wanting to understand the gay and lesbian community. It means so much to me. But those lesbians…I'm fairly certain they were having a brown bag lunch social to meet and hook up with other lesbians…not to hang out with a middle-aged, white man." A few moments of silence were quickly followed with laughter. Apparently, the brown bag lunch lesbians, my "homosexual" homies, had welcomed him as their honorary lesbian. Well played, Dad.

The following holiday, we were all together sitting around the dinner table. It was one of the first times I was with my entire family as a now "out lesbian." But if anyone was concerned, they certainly didn't show it. We were having tacos and it seemed like business as usual with all of us vying for the hot sauce and cheese. In the most serious tone I could muster, I announced to Dad and Geri, "I think with everything that's happened to me and the obvious harder life I've had to endure compared to all of you, I deserved a car. I mean, I'm *gay*." Casually pointing around the table, I added, "You all have no idea what it's been like."

All momentum stopped and the room went silent. I was of course screwing around, pretending to prey on any straight guilt they may have been carrying. Straight people sometimes feel awful for past homophobic comments, or things they think they should have done to help. But I was seriously just fucking around like we've all done for years with one another.

After a long awkward moment, I wasn't sure if *they* knew I was joking. I mean I was most likely the first openly gay women they knew so…shit, maybe they really were carrying some sort of straight guilt? Breaking the silence, Dad reached over for another taco and casually said, "I'll give you a lift in *my* car to the bus stop, honey." Laughter erupted from the table. It felt good to be home.

ELEVEN

DIESEL IN DENIAL

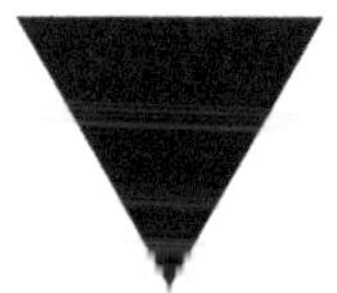

T hough I had finally blown the hinges off my closet door, what I soon discovered was that living as an out butch lesbian, was easier said than done. I had started to openly embrace my sexual orientation and "butchness," which in turn quickly attracted negative attention from the public. I'd inadvertently become a much bigger threat to homophobes, especially men, by not hiding my "abomination." They saw a big, masculine-looking woman as an "in-your-face" threat to their heteronormative way of life. Just because *I'd* had an overall positive and welcoming coming out experience, didn't mean America had. Full acceptance was still elusive, as people seemed more inclined to tolerate us but not embrace us as equal, *normal* members of society.

I'd had a lifetime of playing down my boy-like characteristics. Constantly attempting to conceal any masculine tendencies by wearing makeup and feminine clothing, always styling my hair appropriately long. I'd felt like an imposter pretending to be so overtly feminine. Yet, I never felt excessively masculine either. My gender expression had always fluctuated like a pendulum back and forth, never settling on one end or the other. Once I came out and was allowed to embrace my more masculine side openly, I morphed into what Amy called a "soft butch," merging my masculine and feminine traits. Yet even with my newly found confidence thanks to Amy and a small queer community by my side, I still felt like a butterfly trying to come out of its cocoon in the middle of a hurricane. I just wanted people to see me, to see past my outward appearance and accept me for who I was. Or really, who I'd always been.

It's difficult to explain what it was like carrying the weight of always being on guard, while at the same time wanting so badly to fit in and find acceptance. There I was, embracing my masculinity openly and apparently in society's face, while also fearful of rejection from that same culture. I felt like a walking contradiction. All my life I'd been told I was abnormal, that there was something wrong with me and the way I looked. I was tired yet also angry, being in the spotlight simply for being me. And suddenly, I was even more noticeable—clocked as a big butch lesbian everywhere I went. It was a lot of attention for all the wrong reasons. A kind of aggressive attention, like a gazelle living amongst lions.

There was no predetermined path for gay people then. In fact, I'd never seen an example of a healthy same-sex relationship that I could turn to for guidance. Nothing in our culture said being gay was acceptable. So, Amy and I forged through, carving out our own way of loving one another. We didn't fit the heteronormative narrative of what constituted a proper and appropriate relationship. Honestly, why the fuck would we even *want* to model our lives and relationships after straight people? These were same people who told us anything outside their standard was unacceptable.

I'd been considered a second-class citizen from the day I was born lesbian, never afforded the same equal protection under the law as my straight family and friends. In the eyes of this country, I was seen as mentally and socially disturbed, and undeserving of the same rights as other citizens. If I did find a woman I wanted to share my life with, the idea of getting married was obscene. Even my peanut gallery chimed in at times reminding me, "Women can't marry women!" Yes, the seeds of homophobia had been planted early in my life.

These concepts were so deeply ingrained that eventually, when marriage equality passed, it didn't feel real. I knew intellectually I had won the right to marry a woman, but I'd been brainwashed for so long, it was hard to truly believe I could legally be with a woman. If you tell someone they're less-than long enough, they start to believe it. I did. I assumed I would live my life alone or perhaps with a "companion." To this day, I still remind myself, *I actually can legally marry a woman now.*

My outward expression and appearance had greatly changed, but internally, something else was happening. Along with the new sense of freedom I was feeling, I had unwittingly unleashed a flood of emotions. The outrage and trauma I had been holding in for years began to surface. *How dare anyone tell me who I can love! Fuck them. I have a right to be here, assholes.* Apparently, I was angry. The longer I was out of the closet, surrounded by other gays, the more my resentment grew towards the heteronormative world around me that had done nothing but feed me lie after lie.

Good thing I was attending the University of Oregon, a school known for having plenty of ways to protest. I joined the Gay Club, (which was literally just called the "Gay Club") and began to, let's say, "express" my emotions. I marched, I screamed, and was obnoxiously confrontational with anyone who dared object to me as an out lesbian. I found myself secretly hoping someone might say something derogatory just so I could unleash a torrent of anger.

One time, Amy and I were holding hands just outside of campus when two men passed us. Both looked like they were fresh from some sort of rodeo, sporting massive silver belt buckles and cowboy hats. "Fucking dykes," mumbled one, softly but clear enough to hear. Immediately I turned and shouted, "What the hell did you say?" I was ridiculously puffed-out, like some deranged porcupine. There was a slight moment of hesitation from one of the men, but the other grabbed his arm and led him away. Clearly, I was struggling to contain my simmering rage. *Um, how about some anger management counseling there, Anger Annie?* commented my peanut gallery, noting my borderline overreaction. It had also apparently named my anger "Annie."

The lens with which I viewed the world had changed. I no longer wanted to be a passive victim, watching, hoping not to be noticed. Everything seemed sharper, more focused, as if I was finally seeing just how deeply unfair and fucked up the world around me was. I was no longer a child or teenager having to take it. And I was done hiding and asking for permission to be myself, or for approval of who I was allowed to love. Even if the world shunned me, I was going to live my life openly. Of course, my freshly discovered bravado only invited more unwanted attention.

That summer, Amy and I headed to a popular lake outside of Eugene. The beach was covered with all sorts of obvious straight families, children, and young hormonal teenagers. The tension was palpable from the moment we, the lesbians, arrived. A patchwork quilt of colorful towels and blankets stretched along the shoreline, covered with half naked people in their swim gear, all soaking up the sun. Sweat beaded on my forehead as we made our way through the crowd, and it wasn't from the hot sun. I could feel the weight of their stares as we tiptoed through the maze of people, knowing we were the topic of conversation.

As we passed one particularly large group, I heard laughter and inaudible chatter. I may have been at my tipping point with anger, but I knew better than to stop. I was smart enough not to pick a fight when I was completely outnumbered. I'd dealt with so many overt and subtle forms of homophobic shit, I knew sometimes it was better to just keep moving. "Maybe they *aren't* laughing at us?" I thought, trying to convince myself it was me just being overly sensitive.

We carefully stepped around the sunbathers, not wanting to draw even more attention by stumbling on top of someone's picnic. It was obvious we were the lesbian couple at the beach, not only by our appearance but also by the way we interacted. You know, the way straight couples act in public: walking close together, holding hands, possibly kissing. I could feel my temperature rising even more, incensed by the injustice of it all. It just burned my butt that when straight couples displayed a hint of public affection, they were adorable lovers. Yet when we wanted to simply hold hands, we were a public embarrassment. "They're always so 'in-our-face' with their sexuality," was something I heard all the time.

Feeling completely in the spotlight, my face reddened and hands started shaking slightly, but I kept smiling as I spread out our blanket. Jokingly I said quietly to Amy, "We forgot our 'The Dykes are Here' sign. How is anyone going to know we're gay?" She gave me a sideways smile, like she did so often, silently letting me know, "You're such a dork, but I love you." The entire scene reminded me of an old western, when someone bursts through swinging bar doors and the music abruptly stops and everyone stares. I wanted to scream, "What the fuck are you all looking at, you assholes?!" But Anger Annie was fully in check. All we wanted was to enjoy the beautiful day like everyone else.

We sat there with our legs stretched out, watching water-skiers' slice through the water, ignoring everyone around us to the best of our abilities. Amy had an uncanny ability to literally not notice people. It was like some sort of blind spot superpower she could put up whenever obnoxious assholes were around. In reality, it wasn't that she *couldn't* see douchebag bigots, she just chose to ignore them. I, on the other hand, fucking saw them all the time, unable to ignore them, never knowing if that was a blessing or curse.

I decided to try and take the high road like Amy. "Fuck 'em," I said to myself. And really, although we were gawked at like pariahs, I hadn't actually heard anyone directly say anything. I sensed and felt it, but honestly wasn't certain anything had been said.

Out of nowhere, two women came up, knelt close to our blanket, and began to apologize. We both stared back with blank faces, having no idea what they were talking about. It turned out they were with that group we'd passed, laughing loudly. The same group I'd been trying to convince myself were just obnoxious, drunk people having fun in the sun. My gut was always right. It'd take me years to trust it, but it was always fucking spot on. I guess I just didn't want to accept it. Just once, I wanted to believe we weren't the target.

The women's faces were flushed, clearly embarrassed by their friend's rude behavior. "We're so sorry," one said, as her friend nodded in agreement, quickly adding, "We don't agree with them and would never treat people like that." I could feel my own face flush as we thanked them for their kindness. My first thought was, "What did they call us this time?"

As they walked away, I sat perfectly still, feeling even more self-conscious than before. My throat began to constrict as tears threatened to pour out. I wanted nothing more than to have a long, cathartic cry. Whether it was being targeted by bigots, or called out by sympathetic straight women, there was no avoiding feeling exposed and vulnerable. The crowd either stared and vilified us or they stared at "those poor lesbians" being called pejorative names. And even though someone actually stuck up for us, it was hard to tell if it was out of sympathy or pity? The two often overlap. *"Just fucking leave us alone!"* I thought. All Amy and I had wanted that day was to enjoy a peaceful afternoon at the lake and to—just once—escape the homophobic world around us.

If you're a part of a marginalized group constantly dealing with a hostile world that wants nothing more than to silence and eliminate "your kind," you cling to one another. The 1979 song, "We Are Family" was a perfect gay anthem for a reason. We *were* family. Being called names and treated like freaks of nature took its toll. We had to stick together, just like family would, for protection, support, and the reassurance that there was nothing wrong with being gay. The outside world certainly wasn't going to tell us we were normal and loved. Amy and I clung to one another that day. At a bare minimum we knew, simply by having each other, we were not alone.

For safety, us "birds of a feather did flock together." But we also enjoyed the company of other lesbians. As it turned out, most of us had a lot in common besides our sexual orientation. How *strange*! What made me laugh was how many people outside of the community would say, "You lesbians always congregate in groups." As if lesbians were some wild new species, recently discovered on a *National Geographic* special. I imagined myself leaving for school in the morning and suddenly hearing, in a golf-like whisper, "What you're seeing right now is a *rare* occurrence. Here we have a rather tall, butch lesbian, walking completely alone without her pack. Most lesbian sightings we've witnessed have consisted of three or more, sometimes up to 10 in the group. We think they move like this for protection and, of course, to hunt."

Sitting in the back of my women's studies class one afternoon, the discussion had shifted to why marginalized groups often stick together. A woman had just been attacked on campus, so the conversation evolved to why minorities and women feel uncomfortable alone in certain situations, especially traveling. One lone, muscular, white, straight man named Chad (I'm not shitting you; his name was Chad) stood up to ask a question. He was an ignorant but brave soul to take a course full of almost entirely women, most of whom were just now grasping the depth of their rage towards our sexist culture. Anyway, Chad, dumb or courageous, said, "I don't understand why you women," yes, he said *you* women, "would travel all the way to a foreign country only to hang out with the same kind of people?"

I know what you're thinking, and no, he was not strung up by all the women in the class. But he sure got an earful. My first thought was, *Chad, buddy, you clearly haven't ever been targeted for being the "other." This whole culture was basically built for you and your needs.* I kept my thoughts to myself, as I figured I didn't need to add to the carnage. He was trying, and since our world was one where he was king, he honestly probably didn't understand why we needed to stick together. He most likely never experienced predatory stares, catcalls, or the sting of constant disparaging insults or worse. And based on his outward appearance, he likely hadn't faced much bullying or physical threats. There was safety in numbers for women, and definitely lesbians.

When I was in the company of another lesbian, especially a butch lesbian, there was something very reassuring to me. Without saying one word, I knew her experience. With a simple nod, I had a general idea of the homophobic shit she too, had endured. We shared an unspoken camaraderie, born out of oppression and discrimination. Being together, even in small groups, not only felt safe but also allowed us to be ourselves. We didn't have to explain, educate, or put on the guarded performances we reserved for straight people. We were accepted and loved just as we were. So, yeah, Chad, marginalized groups stuck together because we needed to for safety, and because no one understood the gay experience better than other gays.

That summer, Amy and I decided to go camping. Both of us loved being outdoors but, admittedly, I was a scaredy-cat when it came to overnight camping. Yes, my outwardly tough, imposing butch appearance didn't exactly line up with my internal pussycat. It didn't help that this same year, two lesbians had been attacked by some man while camping in the Appalachian Mountains. One of the women died. It was impossible for us to not be both out-raged and terrified.

When I first heard about it, I was sick to my stomach think-ing about what those poor women went through. I also couldn't escape the reoccurring thought that there wasn't much difference between us and them. It was a stark reminder of how unsafe the world was for gays and lesbians. We tried to put the story out of our minds as we headed out to a similarly remote area.

While loading up our camping gear, I noticed Amy had packed her hunting knife, an enormous Maglite flashlight, rope, an axe, and who-knows-what-else in her olive-green army pack. Just in case we needed to go to battle, I supposed. She was clearly a tougher lesbian than I, and she was always prepared. When set-ting up our tent, she strategically positioned it in such a way that no one could sneak up without us hearing them. This, of course, was for my benefit. On one side of our tent there was a fairly steep drop-off, another butted up against the reservoir, and the third side backed up to a slanted hill covered in tiny pumice-like pebbles that made loud, tumbling sounds when traversed.

All snuggled up in my warm, feather-down sleeping bag, I fell asleep rather quickly, only to wake up an hour later knowing for sure I'd heard something outside. Eyes barely open I told myself it was nothing. *Fucking go to sleep,* I mumbled internally. Then the overly anxious side of my peanut gallery said, "I bet that's what those two lesbians thought right before they were attacked." Now fully awake, I stayed perfectly still, listening for any little noise. Then I heard it. An enormous *CRUNCH*, like someone stepping on a bunch of twigs. When you're in a tent in the middle of the night with thoughts of a maniac lesbian killer flooding your brain, little sounds seem like very, very large ones.

Without missing a beat, I rolled over, covered Amy's mouth with my hand, making sure she wouldn't make a sound, and whis-pered loudly, "Get the knife. There's a man outside our tent." Yeah…I did that. Amy went from a deep, peaceful sleep to sitting straight up, eyes bulging, fully alert and awake. She grabbed her knife and silently unzipped the tent flap, her massive flashlight in tow. I sat for what seemed an eternity, trying to hear her over the deafening thunder sound of my heart hammering my chest.

Sitting in the tent I suddenly thought, *"Well shit, now I'm all alone in here and she's outside with the knife and light!"* then timidly poked my head out to see what was happening. I wasn't sure if she needed help or if I should retreat and hide in my sleeping bag. By the light of the moon and the partial illumination of her flashlight, I saw her standing in her long johns, glaring. At me. "What?" I asked with a hint of feigned incredulity. She pointed her flashlight to the ground, close to the tent. A small, furry grey mouse scurried away in the light. "It was a mouse. A fucking mouse," she stated.

It was becoming clear I *may* have overreacted, but instead of just admitting it, I decided to argue, "No way. I heard someone. Seriously, I did." She sighed and crawled back into the tent. We laid there in the silence, listening to the occasional frog or cricket. Then I started laughing, "OK *maybe* I overreacted. But I swear it sounded much louder." She went on to remind me of her strategic placement of our tent, and how no one could possibly sneak up undetected—except maybe a Navy Seal. Now unable to stop laughing, I said, "By the way, next time it'd be great if in your rush to leave the tent, you left me a flashlight and weapon." Her response was prompt, "There is no way you are getting a weapon."

Because of my size and appearance, people naturally assumed I was tough, both physically and emotionally. This is probably one of the reasons why I was targeted more often by straight men. I understood why, even back then. Aside from other straight men, butch lesbians were probably their biggest threat. Here was this manly looking woman, that *their* "woman" might check out. And I'm assuming they thought somehow, I not only wanted their women but was going to steal them, like they were property. It was some sort of weird macho thing I became part of simply because I was butch. It was ridiculous.

I felt a certain solace when I began to fully realize being born gay had nothing to do with me or my choices. I was who I was. There were plenty of homophobes at the time who said being gay was a "choice." The notion we were choosing our sexual orientation was laughable, yet people really believed it. First of all, I had liked girls ever since I hit puberty. Second, why would anyone choose a life of persecution and pain? It made no sense. It would have been similar to asking someone who claimed to only have attraction towards the opposite sex to "choose" to have sex with the same sex and enjoy it! It was just another narrative the homophobic, heteronormative world tried to spin everything, so it seemed like *I* was the confused, abnormal degenerate in need of fixing.

The deeper it sank in that it was actually the world around me that had major issues with sexual orientation and gender, the clearer my mind became and more validated I felt. A lifetime of shame around being a lesbian was slowly falling away. I also knew my sexual orientation and the way that I presented my gender wasn't simple or two-dimensional. Despite my outward appearance, even if the world assumed I was this tough, *"you-wanna-a-piece-of-me"* diesel dyke, I was just like other people: complex. And I certainly wasn't rough and tough.

Amy loved the term diesel dyke and thought it was hilarious. Stereotypical diesel dykes wore Carhartt and flannel, rode motorcycles, and had faces spattered with grease. I, conversely, did *not* like dirt and might have been considered more of a "GAP dyke" at the time as most of my clothing came from that store. Clean, crisp, and tidy. Amy knew I was the opposite of a rough diesel dyke. She also knew I had hang-ups around my masculine appearance. Amy's idea of helping me push through my own internalized gender issues and homophobia was to jokingly take it to the opposite extreme. Whatever the issue was, she'd make it cringe-worthy, and so loud that I'd eventually give in and laugh. Usually at myself.

Her special spin on this occasion was, "Diesel in denial," as if I simply hadn't realized yet that I was a diesel dyke. In fact, she started her own little singing rhyme that she decided needed to be on loop, something like a commercial jingle you can't get out of your head. "Diesel in deniiiial… Diesel in deniiiial…. Diesel in deniiiial," she'd sing over and over, everywhere we went, emphasizing and elongating the end of "denial" until we both laughed.

Yes, I looked masculine, butch, and tough sometimes. And that was OK. It was also OK that my outward appearance didn't necessarily match my inward personality. More importantly, her jovial teasing did eventually help me overcome years of deeply embedded skewed ideas of gender roles. It helped me realize that yes, it was perfectly acceptable for a female to appear masculine.

One Saturday afternoon we were napping in the back of our rental house. Our landlords, who lived next door, were out of town. It was pleasantly quiet—a perfect day for a nice long snooze. We were almost asleep when we heard a soft knock on our front door. I knew Amy thought it was our landlord Paul, so I whispered, "It's not Paul. He told me he'd be out of town today." Lost in our drowsy summer afternoon state, we ignored the knocks, assuming whoever it was would go away. Then we heard keys jingling, our front door opened, and the living room light turned on. We both shot straight up, perfectly still.

Realizing someone had come inside, we leapt up, frantically trying to untangle our twisted sheets, and peered around our bedroom door. Taking the lead, Amy tiptoed through the kitchen toward the lighted front room, me clinging to her. Like an oversized shadow, I hovered behind as we peeked around the kitchen into the front room. Standing side by side, we looked like David and Goliath. She was this lean, lanky, tiny thing compared to me, yet her bravado certainly compensated for her smaller stature. I on the other hand, was this tall, bulky woman who was seriously wondering why we were creeping towards the *front* door instead of running out the *back*.

To our horror, we saw a giant. A towering man in a black leather jacket with matching pants, whose head almost touched the ceiling, was rummaging through our front drawers, randomly picking through our things. Unfortunately for him, in his massive pumpkin sized hands, he was clutching Amy's beloved Maglite and leather vest. Big mistake. Her prized possessions. While Amy was realizing what he was holding, I was standing there stunned, unable to take my eyes off the size of this guy. And his hands! They were fucking huge! She moved towards him while I turned the other way thinking, *Run away!*

Without an ounce of hesitation, Amy steam rolled into the living room, screaming both physically and verbally, "What the fuck are you doing? Get the fuck outta here!" He turned, in shock, and instantly recoiled, stuttering something about trying to give back the keys that were in the door. "Bullshit!" She yelled as she snatched her things and our keys out of his hands. Before he knew what hit him, Amy and her little body had shoved the giant man out the door.

I stood there alone in the kitchen doorway, my mouth agape in shock—and a little turned on. But then immediately back to shock. "What the hell did I just witness?" I continued, laughing nervously, "Holy shit. Did you just push that giant man outside with your little body, while reading him the riot act?"

All of it felt unreal. When my heartbeat finally began to rev down, all I could do was laugh. Itty-bitty Amy saved the day while big butch "diesel dyke" Shaley stood there, weighing her options. Of which there was one: run out the back door, scream for help, and make sure all my teeth remained intact. I rushed into the living room to her side, all puffed up, letting her know, "I got you babe," while I relocked the front door. With her Maglite and vest reclaimed, she stared at me with a familiar look of disbelief. Then I looked down at her hands and said, "Oh hey, *there* are my keys!"

TWELVE
SLEEPING MONSTERS

Amy and I were at the local queer bar waiting for friends. I'd downed a few beers before going inside because I was, well, scared. Being out and engaging in the LGBT community was a new world to me. One with different categories of how to look and behave. Especially for butch lesbians. There was a certain unsaid expectation from the queer culture that we were supposed to be sexy yet tough, void of emotion. I'm guessing it was unconsciously modeled after the established heteronormative idea of how straight men were perceived. Even being a "soft" butch as Amy had called me, I was still labeled "butch." This was the mid-1990's and a distinct binary between masculinity and femininity still existed, even amongst queers. With lesbians, there wasn't much flexibility or give when it came to identity. You fell somewhere in the realm of butch or femme.

Already feeling the buzz of beers I'd consumed in the car before coming in, the first thing I did was march up to the bar for more. My heart was nervously pounding in rhythm with the club music that pulsated a heavy dance beat over and over. It was all a show. I'd sort of traded one world of pretend for another. I leaned my back against the bar while I waited for our drinks wearing my bomber leather jacket and sunglasses, trying to appear cool. George Michael's *Faith* album was popular and I'm fairly certain I was aiming for a George Michael look-a-like. *"You look ridiculous. Is this your attempt at looking studly?"* commented my peanut gallery barely audible over the thumping music. "Gotta have faith," I replied allowing a breath of comic relief to help ease my overly tensed nerves.

I was doing the best I could. Trying to find my place and mirror my new crowd. More masculine lesbians in our community acted stoic, drank, and seemed a whole lot tougher than me. And it was painful to watch how awful and awkward I was at playing bar games. If another woman flirted with me, was I supposed to nod? Did I ignore her like, "I've got a woman, babe, move on." It was confusing and I had to laugh at the circular nature of it all. One minute I'm unsure how to act straight, the next I'm confused how to act gay. But no matter how uncomfortable I felt in my new, freshly ironed "tough" butch skin, it was still a thousand times more comfortable than pretending to be straight.

I drank before coming out to fit in and numb my suffering. I drank *after* coming out to also fit in and numb a different kind of suffering. Alcohol was my oil can to the Tin Man; it loosened everything up. It made me forget my closeted years, and then helped me feel attractive, and somewhat cool and accepted after I came out. It was imperative, or at least it felt that way, that I fit in with my new queer friends. Where would I go if *this* crowd didn't accept me? I mean, shit, I was running out of groups to belong too. And although my heart wasn't bearing the weight of deep loneliness from being closeted anymore, a new part of me, or perhaps a part of me I was seeing for the first time, was having to confront a more public, overt type of homophobia, not to mention my own internalized homophobia.

Predictably over time, my drinking started to bleed into all areas of my life and became harder to control. Vice-gripping hangovers often kept me from work and school. Friends were embarrassed, and often pissed, after witnessing my drunken debauchery at parties or clubs, bumping into tables and knocking over chairs. I was either passing out on people's couches, sometimes blacking out, having no memory of the night before. And I was an angry drunk. *Surprise!* Yes, I was argumentative, volatile, and mouthy. It was as if 'Anger Annie' got a free pass to do or say anything when I was inebriated. But at some point in my years of trying to control my anxiety, fear and loneliness with alcohol; it began to control me.

One evening after returning from the bar late, I told Amy in barely comprehensible, slurred speech, "I *knooow* you like that woman!" Some woman at the bar had dared to look at Amy. I'd been droning on and on about her for a while. It usually went that way, me drunk on some soap box spewing some long-winded fucked up monologue, never really having any proof or much of a point. "You're drunk. Go to sleep," was all she said while taking off my jeans and shoving me onto the bed. I know what you're thinking, nothing screams sex appeal more than a person who's constantly falling down drunk, transparently insecure, disheveled and loudly accusatory.

Then one morning, after a lifetime of coexisting with my alcohol pal, I woke up with a particularly harsh mind-numbing hangover, looked in my mirror through blood-shot eyes and said, "Enough." That's right, I literally just decided to stop. It was the classic idiom of a "lightbulb going off" in my brain. It just clicked. Standing there, head pounding, I realized to my core I had to stop. Alcohol was poison to my mind and body, and I was clearly unable to control it. I never went to meetings or picked up a book about addiction. I just stopped.

Slowly my life began to improve. I lost weight, my complexion cleared, and I had a ridiculous amount of energy. Standing in front of the mirror one morning, I noticed the jeans I put on that hadn't fit me for years, suddenly looked fantastic. "How *you* doin'?" I said to my reflection while pointing and winking.

Yet with all the upsides, it also felt strange walking away from something that'd been a crutch for years. I'd woven alcohol into my daily life. It was part of me. Suddenly gone, I felt like I'd lost a piece of who I was—searching for my phantom limb. I was ending a bitter-sweet "relationship" I'd had with alcohol for over a decade. But let's face it, the "bitter" part had been contaminating everything and the people around me for far too long. Often acting the fool and pushing away the people I loved. What I didn't realize after quitting so seemingly easy, was that alcohol was not my drug of choice. I hadn't even heard the term, "drug of choice". More importantly, I had absolutely no knowledge about the disease of addiction, and certainly no understanding that it doesn't simply go away.

The downside of sobriety was without the numbing effects of alcohol, I soon discovered how completely unaware and naïve I was to the depth of my emotional and psychological scars. I'd had a lifetime of hiding in a world that seemed to be disgusted by my mere existence, and a childhood spent navigating the insanity of my mother's instability. None of these deeply rooted issues miraculously disappeared simply because I stopped drinking, found love and came out. In fact, without the numbing effects of alcohol, they became impossible to ignore.

I had a monster of sorts, one that developed at a young age to protect me. It was born out of anger and injustice, there to defend and guard me from the outside world and, sadly, my own mother. There I was after drinking, thinking my life was finally on an upward, calm trajectory, and I had become somewhat emotionally and mentally stable. I was unaware that my insecurities and anger were still fully intact and not planning on leaving anytime soon. My protective monster had simply gone dormant.

Growing up, my mother had imprinted upon me certain ideas. People were untrustworthy and love was elusive, and if I did find love it certainly wouldn't last. If I wanted to keep people around, I needed to be guarded and fight for them to stay. Love was very much a piece of pie. Not everyone could have it and if you were lucky enough to find a piece, someone would try to steal it from you. All of these ideas reinforced the erroneous belief that I was not worthy of love. I knew if someone stayed long enough to see the real me, they would leave. It was such a strange contradictory existence, desperately longing to be loved and included, yet so full of fear that I pushed anyone daring to love me away.

What is it about the connection between children and parents that runs far deeper than any other relationship? Even intimate, romantic relationships—while strong and profound—are nothing compared to the parent-child bond. Those are the ones that make or break us. Although my father was a shining example of unconditional love and unwavering stability, my mother was the opposite and ended up damaging me the most. There was little reliability, no consistency, and a list of unsaid rules around the dispensing of love. Especially when it came to my father. If I defended or spoke highly of him, her love and attention vanished. "Come on, Mom. Dad isn't that bad. No one's that bad," I said after one of her "Chuck is evil" rants. Her face immediately contorted into a disgusted glare, as if I'd just committed a horrible crime. And each time afterwards, I'd feel a ripple of shame and fear course through my body—even as an adult.

When I was younger, I often had no clue what I'd done to set her off. It was like a game of "Who is Mom this time?" Sometimes when she was around, she'd simply ignore me. Physically she was there, but not at all present. Other times, she'd be overly loving, focused, doting on me as if I was her favorite child. "You are so witty and bright, Shaley. Always my smart one!" she'd praise. And she meant it. I could feel authentic devotion and kindness behind her words.

But within a short amount of time, I'd receive a completely different Mom. Out of nowhere, she'd barge into my room yelling about insignificant, trivial things, "The dishes aren't done! Get up and do them now!" I became numb to it over the years. I mean, it wasn't as extreme as *Mommy Dearest* but strangely similar in her unstable patterns. Her erratic behavior led me to feeling on edge constantly, to the point where I eventually became rude and dismissive in my responses, "Seriously, Mom! Just go away," I'd snap back.

There was no logic. She was a brilliant, kind-hearted woman with serious psychological issues. Her emotional roller coaster felt extremely dangerous, so I'd unconsciously learned never to get too close. Her unpredictability became predictable. She couldn't hurt me if I closed down emotionally and shut her out. The problem, of course, is closing that door closed me in. When I started shutting her out at an early age, I shut my emotions down. I know— tick, tock, motherfucker.

Top off those twisted, dysfunctional lessons with years of being closeted and judged for being gay, and you've got one majorly confused, hurt human being. Needless to say, I carried a constant undercurrent of apprehension and skepticism into all relationships, especially my intimate ones. I masqueraded about as a tough, impenetrable butch lesbian, when underneath I was a scared, untrusting little girl, often seething with insecurity and jealousy. Lucky Amy!

I found myself behaving like an unhinged person, badgering Amy constantly, "Who was that on the phone?" "Where did you meet her?" "Why is she calling so late?" It was nuts. I was continually making erroneous, sometimes fantastical accusations and exhibiting fairly creepy, stalker-like behavior. I had no reservoir of trust and why would I? I'd never experienced what it was like to trust. My perspective was simple; people say they love you, then they lie and hurt you, then they leave. The problem with the insidious nature of jealousy is I ended up pushing away the one thing I wanted so desperately. It was a vicious, cyclical, self-fulfilling prophecy. There's nothing like pummeling your partner with never-ending false allegations. That's the quickest way to get someone to move away from you, not cuddle up close.

I became two different people. One was a grown, mature, confident adult, running my own business, paying bills, having dinner parties, and so on. But when it came to intimacy and relationships, I transformed into a petulant, overgrown, immature child. I would literally have meltdowns, like a kid in the middle of the grocery store, not getting the candy bar I wanted. Except my meltdowns came from deep, ominous, fear-based insecurities instead of a child in desperate need of a nap. It was embarrassing.

My actions felt almost out of my control, as if I was outside observing my irrational behavior in disbelief, but not understanding how to stop. Like there was some other me who took over and turned the adult into a clingy, overly dramatic, controlling asshole. And lord, the circular nature of it all was exhausting. Accusations, fighting, crying, feeling out of control, pleading for another chance, making up, accusations...and so forth.

After we got into an argument, I would fall into a sea of despair, assuming Amy would leave me. I would loop self-loathing stories, "Of course she'll leave you. Why on God's green earth would someone like that want *you*?" or "What did you expect, you fucking loser? Any other lesbian would be better than you." Really wholesome, fun-loving stuff.

It's surprising to me that Amy, and the other women I've been with, not only stayed with me but actually put up with my bullshit. But no one talked much then about jealousy and the insidious destruction it causes to both individuals and couples.

I also realized I still held an enormous amount self-hatred and anger from my own internalized homophobia. Boiling like an underground dilapidated tunnel of steam, starting to crack from years of neglect. I'd repeatedly heard directly, or in conversation, a plethora of derogatory, homophobic comments ever since I was young. You really do start to believe the lies you're told, even if those lies are about you. The commentary around lesbians was usually categorized. There were hot "femme" lesbians and then disgusting mannish ones. Hello, butch Shaley.

For straight men, lesbians who appeared more stereotypically feminine (i.e., long hair, generally smaller, curvaceous physiques, and big boobs) were hot. You know, porn lesbians. That was what women who were gay were "supposed" to look like. I don't recall ever knowing a ton of real lesbians that looked that way. I'm sure there were extremely feminine looking lesbians surrounding me, but I wouldn't have been able to pick one out to save my life. Then there were the masculine lesbians like me, who were abnormal freaks, confused and just wanted to be men. Oh, and we all had "penis envy."

One evening at dusk, while I was walking home, a group of men wearing backwards baseball hats and sporting thick flannel shirts, started heckling me from across the street. One guy laughed while he grabbed his crotch, shouting, "Missing your dick, lesbo?" Then he looked back at his buddies, cracking up. I have no idea what happened to me in that instant. Maybe it was years of being called names? But I'd had enough. I was pissed. I yelled back, "First of all, my dick is *huge*, ask your wife. And mine's in the shape of a giant *dolphin*, asshole!"

My peanut gallery exploded with raucous applause. It wasn't often I ever had any sort of decent response in confrontational situations. Immediately, however, I regretted the "my dick is dolphin shaped" part. It sort of ruined the whole "fuck you I'm tough" vibe I was going for. Despite that bit of overshare, though, I was still elated. In most hostile situations, any wit I possessed vanished. Usually, I struggled to even respond with complete sentences. More often than not, I simply wouldn't have the guts to respond at all, as there were three of them and one of me.

My comeback caught him off guard, as I'm sure he wasn't expecting any resistance with his buddies close by. He became enraged and belligerent, and I heard a deluge of grotesque and demeaning insults spew from his mouth, ending with, "You're a disgusting fucking dyke who needs to be locked up in a mental institution." I couldn't tell if his buddies felt ashamed, but they both stopped laughing and gracefully convinced him to walk away. I walked away too, in the opposite direction, heavily shaking from adrenaline. I was contemplating his comment while angry tears began to fall. *I wouldn't be surprised growing up in this fucking culture if I did end up in an institution, thanks to assholes like you.*

These types of interactions served as a brutal reminder that gays and lesbians would not be accepted in America anytime soon. Something apparently the world would not let me forget. Even though I was finding my voice, I felt like a walking contradiction. Letting go of a lifetime of societally imposed shaming was easier said than done. I was slowly starting to overcome my internalized homophobia and truly love myself authentically. But then, I'd find myself—seemingly out of nowhere—feeling disgusted by all things, other lesbians. Especially butch ones. Yes, my *own* butch sisters.

It had been so deeply ingrained in me that masculine looking lesbians were such freakish aberrations, when I saw others in public, my first reaction was repulsion. "Ugh, she is so gross. Why doesn't she try and wear more form-fitting clothing?" I'd mutter to Amy as we passed. She would look at me with shocked amazement. "Um, you are just like her." I'd look back in disbelief and claim there was no way in hell I looked anything like that butch. It was laughable, and at the same time, extraordinarily sad. I *was* exactly like her but couldn't see how deep my own self-hatred ran. It would take me years to undo the lies I believed and fully embrace—and love—my own masculinity. And other butch lesbians.

THIRTEEN

MY GOOD PAL VICODIN

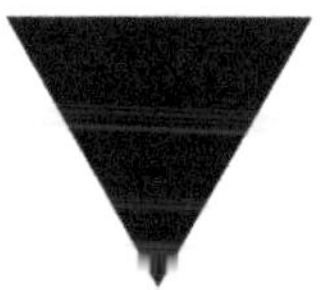

As my college years came to an end, my pill problem hadn't fully embedded itself in my life but was dancing on the peripheral edges. They were a once-every-three-month kind of party. If there was an upcoming weekend where I knew I'd be alone, my strategizing mind would excitedly begin to create a plan for scoring pills. *Just to relax*, I'd tell myself convincingly. *What's the big deal? Everyone has some sort of crutch in life. I deserve a staycation.*

Since I had stopped drinking a few years prior without much difficulty, I assumed I was clean and sober. Everyone, including myself, had been surprised how easily I had simply stopped drinking after years of uncontrollable drunkenness. Alcohol had been the major disrupting problem in my life, not the occasional pill popping. So, when it came to painkillers, I told myself that, just like drinking, I could always drop it whenever I wanted. It was just a few pills every now and then. What serious harm could they do? I had a successful career, a wonderful partner, and even a dog. Shit, everything was perfect. *I'll just have a little mellow weekend all by myself with my pal Vicodin.*

Getting painkillers was a piece of cake back in the 1990s. Fall down and need stitches? Doctors prescribed some sort of opioid. Have your wisdom teeth pulled? Opioids. Sprain your ankle? Opioids. Really, for any kind of injury, as long as I complained about the pain, doctors would prescribe—that's right—opioids. That was their answer to everything. The insane addictive nature of it all was rarely, if ever, discussed—at least in the beginning.

As soon as my staycation weekend began, I'd head straight to the local ER, playing the poor injured bird perfectly. I'd walk awkwardly through the sliding hospital doors with a deliberately slow gait, pretending that I'd re-injured my back. While waiting, I'd make sure to sit up as rigid and upright as possible, wincing occasionally at my imaginary pain, just in case anyone was secretly watching. I had no problem at all waiting there for hours if that's what it took.

Eventually I'd hear a questioning, "Shaley?" and stiffly make my way over to the nurse waiting with my file. "Right here," I'd say in a phony, unsteady, pain-induced tone and slowly follow as they led me back to one of the examination rooms. "Please remove your clothes and put on this gown. The doctor will be in shortly," they'd instruct as I settled into the tiny, cold room. I'd hear a heavy click as the door closed, then happily strip, and put on the folded blue paper.

Sometimes I'd sit in those sterile rooms for hours, fidgeting with my paper gown, trying to cover my naked body and keep warm. Being that it was the emergency hospital, each person's level of urgency was triaged, and back pain wasn't always considered a top priority. I didn't care, nor did I ever argue with anyone about how long it was taking. They were the gatekeepers of my drug. Plus, in addition to actually taking painkillers, there was always a fucked-up rush that came from the chase and all the anticipation and scheming. The end game of consuming the pills was ecstasy, but the process of getting them was also strangely thrilling.

By the time a doctor came in to ask me what happened, where it hurt and how long it had been going on, I was running on pure adrenaline. *It's happening, Shaley! Just be cool and keep up the good act.* The doctor would start to scribble something down on their pad. "Have you ever had Vicodin? It'll make you a little drowsy so make sure you take it at home and with lots of water," they'd say. I'd nod in compliance while feeling a rush of energy course through me. Immediately after the doctor left, I'd scan the prescription for the quantity, calculating how long could I ride my narcotic magic carpet

First stop? Pharmacy. As soon as I had those pills in hand, I'd grab whatever bottle of water was rolling around in my car and inhale them. The combination of chasing the drug, topped off with consuming them, left me in pure climax bliss. Like the clickity-clack of a world-class roller coaster ride, it inches you up and up. You're teetering on the precipice for what feels like an eternity, body tingling with anticipation, and you sneak a glance over the edge. Then *whoosh*, you're thrust over and soaring down the rails, body airborne and stomach in your throat. Un-fucking-believable.

After the thrill of seeking and finding pills was over, I'd head home for the next phase of my opioid adventure. It was time to float and vegetate on my couch. I'd sit there for hours watching TV, counting out my pills to calculate how many hours (possibly days) I'd have to ride my high—alone. "Ah, this is the life," I'd say out loud. I'd eat and zone out with my drug pal, feeling as if my life was complete instead of realizing that it was slowly falling apart. My numbing brain and detached body easily convinced me all was well. Yet the cracks on my delusional façade were spreading.

Since coming out, I thought my problems, for the most part, were behind me. I was no longer hiding my sexual orientation and mistakenly thought my childhood traumas were directly somehow connected to years of being closeted. Prior to coming out, I had deeply believed no one would love me. But then someone did come along who—surprise—loved me. I was certain I had figured out who Shaley Howard was. Someone overflowing with self-love and inner confidence, who'd shed years of shame. I thought I'd fully embraced my butch masculinity and sexual orientation, marching and proudly proclaiming, "I'm Here! I'm Queer! Get used to it!" in every Pride parade.

The problem was, I never paused long enough to consider that if all of this supposed self-actualization was real and I had truly overcome my internal issues, why was I still seeking drugs? My naivety and ignorance around emotional and psychological trauma, combined with having no understanding of the complexities of addiction, had me steamrolling blindfolded into dangerous, uncharted territory.

I'd used alcohol for years to deny my feelings of inadequacy, always trying to numb myself. Still, I never made the connection between alcohol and pills. Over-drinking led to alcoholism; we didn't call it an addiction. It wasn't the same as being an addicted to drugs. Drug addicts were hyped-up coke users or meth-heads, certainly not people who used prescription drugs. They were fictional characters I'd see in movies, usually found dead in a squalor, dilapidated house with a needle sticking out of their arm. It never dawned on me that alcohol might also have been a seriously addictive and dangerous drug. And I certainly never equated Vicodin with being a drug. I mean hell, doctors prescribed it. Why would they prescribe anything so addictive and possibly fatal?

The gravity of my situation clearly hadn't hit home yet. Any occasional passing thoughts around becoming addicted to Vicodin were immediately ignored and dismissed. *I don't need them, I want them. Big difference. They are just for fun and only on special occasions,* I'd think, attempting to reassure myself that I wasn't perilously close to sliding down the rabbit hole. But it had started to feel like a mindfuck, trying to differentiate between true bodily pain and some twisted addict's head game, urging me to believe I was feeling pain that wasn't there. My intellect and voice of reason became clouded and confused as it subtly whispered, "Why can't two plus two equal five?"

Then my back took a turn for the worse, and the intense sporadic pain became almost a daily problem. The line between wanting and needing painkillers merged. The hospitals at that time hadn't quite recognized how massive the opioid crisis was, so getting pills was still relatively easy. The internet was also fairly new, so connecting hospital databases with other hospitals in order to identify "pill-seeking behavior" was challenging. Trying to fool the hospitals wasn't my concern, however, since suddenly I wasn't faking; the pain was real and growing exceedingly intolerable.

One time, while at the ER (for actual pain) a kind and overly concerned doctor took one look at my contorted face and suggested I have another MRI. This time around, the resulting image was noticeably different. Apparently, there was supposed to be space between all of my spinal vertebrae, little pillowy cushions in between the bones that allow us to walk with ease. My L1 and L2 vertebrae had no such cushion. My disc was completely ruptured and flat. Even the doctor looked a bit surprised. Hello, back surgery! After years of not seeing any evidence to prove I was indeed in pain, I felt somewhat vindicated. I wanted to shout, "I told you!" But then the addict took over and exclaimed silently, *Holy shit, we're gonna get so many drugs!*

Only when you seriously injury certain parts of your body do you appreciate how important and useful that particular part is in daily activities. Back injuries are an absolute nightmare. Even the simplest things, like walking my dog or bending over to pick up laundry, were excruciating. Every fucking thing I tried to do.

I was eager for surgery and putting an end to my pain. But when the surgeons explained how invasive and complicated the process was, I sat there dumbfounded. They needed to go in through my abdomen and literally set aside my internal organs in order to access and replace the broken disc. At the time, they didn't have the expertise to go through the backside without the possibility of damaging a nerve. Once they were in and able to remove my ruptured disc, they would fuse my bones back together with titanium implants.

I remember reading through a litany of procedural materials covering everything from details of the surgery to the recovery process. At the end of the pamphlet, I found one short paragraph warning of the dangers of painkillers. That was it. Page after page detailing the surgery was followed by one measly paragraph about opioids. Still, it was the first real professional bit of information that warned me of the extremely addictive nature of these drugs. I, of course, skimmed it, and then proceeded to ignore it. I knew I loved the effects of these drugs and wasn't anywhere close to believing I was an addict.

The morning of my surgery, I was laying on a gurney next to three other patients. We were all lined up, side by side in a small, white, very quiet room. It felt like a sci-fi holding corral. "We look like comatose human cattle lining up for the slaughter," I joked, breaking the silence and cracking myself up. The other three just stared at me like I had already sampled the happy drugs.

Seemingly out of nowhere, a tall, masked man wearing blue rubber gloves—who I *think* was the anesthesiologist—leaned over and asked if I wanted a spinal block in addition to the general anesthesia. In the never-ending paperwork I'd read, I had missed the pre-surgery, anesthetic part of the program. Unsure, but not wanting any additional pain, I agreed. He smiled, poked me with something, and I was out like a light.

The next thing I knew, I was trying to pry open my eyes and understand the muffled, incoherent voices surrounding me. I knew I was in the recovery room, but everything was disorienting, and I had no memory of the whole ordeal. (Except my cow joke.) There was no cool out of body or tragic near-death experience for me. I was awake, then I wasn't, then I was awake again.

Through blurred vision, I saw a nurse hovering over me. She checked my vitals and informed me the surgery went well. Still unable to form words, I made my mouth smile. I think. I'm not entirely sure what my face was doing. She reached down and kindly wiped my drool.

I then found myself half-awake in a hospital bed, not certain how I'd magically arrived. My first thought? *I can't feel my legs.* Fear escalated as I tried to reach down and touch them but felt nothing. I started flailing about, yelling, "I can't feel my legs! I can't feel my fucking legs!" I knew it. I knew the doctor would nick my nerve and paralyze me. I would learn later that this was because the spinal block was still working and the transition to the morphine drip hadn't been completed. I (temporarily) couldn't feel anything from my waist down.

Suddenly, multiple nurses were surrounding my bed, all trying to desperately calm me down and remind me about the spinal block. I continued to spiral into a full throttle panic attack, screaming. My dad and my friend, both waiting outside my room, told me later they could hear me all the way at the end of the hallway.

But for fuck's sake! The anesthesiologist could've explained the difference between general anesthesia and a spinal block *before* I went in for a surgery that had the possibility, a rare possibility but possibility none-the-less, that could result in me being paralyzed. In my mind, I'd woken up after going under the knife, had no recollection of detailed conversations about anesthesia options, and could no longer feel my legs. "Oh, by the way, if we give you a spinal block you won't feel half of your body when you wake up," might have been helpful. Although in hindsight, it may have been in the pre-surgery packet of information I skimmed.

The next few weeks were pure agony. The transition of pain from surgery wasn't bad, but lying flat on my back, staring up at my ceiling was torturous. Every day was the same thing. I read, slept, and popped painkillers. The days blended one into another and as I healed, the line between real pain and "I want to get high" pain, once again, started to blur. The doctor had prescribed an insane amount of Vicodin—it should have lasted for months. I had blown through them enthusiastically, knowing in the back of my addict brain that there would be plenty of refills.

One day, soon after returning home, instead of waiting for someone to pick up my refill, I decided to get it myself. Did the doctors *all* explicitly tell me to lay flat on my back as much as possible for at least six weeks? Yes. Would they have vehemently chastised me for moving more than necessary? Absolutely. Did the addict in me ignore all of their advice and any sliver of common sense I possessed, chalking it up to a simple *suggestion*? Of course. I wanted my drug and wanted it right then.

Driving to get more drugs when my bones weren't fused completely was one of the dumbest decisions I'd ever made. This was on top of a lifetime of mountains of ridiculous, idiotic choices. That's how addiction rolls. I somehow convinced myself it was safe, even though I could have permanently damaged my back, or paralyzed myself by hitting a pothole. Even worse, I could've ended up in an accident and hurt someone else.

Red flags, flying left and right, were becoming harder to ignore. Despite my attempts at living obliviously, it was quickly becoming terrifyingly clear I would go to great lengths for my drug habit. And yes, let's face it, it was now a habit. My mind continued to resist and rationalize, while a growing voice inside was screaming the truth. I just kept repeating to myself, "I am not an addict." I needed the drugs for my back pain, and I was still in complete control.

Months after my surgery, a lingering shadow of depression seemed to follow me. The surgery itself ended up being successful. My back worked perfectly, and after completing rigorous physical therapy there wasn't any lasting chronic pain. But I couldn't seem to escape a feeling of unhappiness. I continued to pop pills occasionally, but as I transitioned back into my regular life, the quantity I consumed lessened dramatically. I was still able to control the number of pills I took, which only reinforced my complete denial that I was, in fact, an addict.

Life in a smaller town like Eugene was becoming unbearable. As a recently out lesbian, I longed for a larger queer community. My hometown of Portland seemed to be hollering, "Come up here, honey. We are everywhere!"

It certainly didn't help my situation that Amy had already moved to Portland. Yes, my first true love, and partner of 10 years, was now an ex. My first ex actually. I had fallen head over heels for Amy years ago. But I was also very young, foolish and naïve. Neither of us had wanted to admit our relationship had morphed into friendship and any romantic love we felt had long since vanished. I think in many ways, we stayed together out of fear. It's scary for most people to let go of love relationships, especially your first ones—you know, the one you think will last forever. But it's often terrifying for LGBT because our pool of people to choose from is simply smaller. There may be ample choices in the straight world, but not so much in the lesbian one. The idea of there being "plenty of other fishes in the sea" wasn't exactly true. Plus, I was petrified at the thought of losing my best friend whom I'd shared so many joyful and monumental experiences with throughout our ten years together.

In the end, however, we just couldn't keep up the romantic façade and had to throw in the towel. I spent a year trying to talk with Amy as much as she would let me, knowing that despite the heartache and pain of the breakup, she *would* be my BFF. I loved her so much and could not imagine my life without her. Also, she had no choice. *"I will just keep showing up anytime she's up for talking like her shadow. A shadow she can't get rid of no matter how hard she tries! She WILL love me! As a friend. My best friend."* I would think constantly.

She eventually fell in love with another woman, and as I predicted, became my bestie. Since we'd been close friends for years, the transition to BFF's wasn't hard. Also, it's pretty typical when lesbians break up to remain friends. Not all the time, but often. It's a lesbian thing. Since our community is small and closely-knit honestly, if we didn't figure out how to get over residual relationship shit, we wouldn't *have* other lesbian friends. So, we learn to slide into friendship zone fast. I'm fairly certain we should get some sort of adaptability award.

Soon after Amy and I broke up, I started dating Jennifer from the office where I worked. She was a stunning, highly intelligent, witty, and might I add, *sexy as all hell*, woman. Unfortunately, it turned out to be a somewhat complicated relationship. Maybe my expectations were too high. Or, given my internal fucked up baggage, it may have been more along the lines of, "It's not you, trust me, it's me." I'm guessing it was a combination of everything at the time. Within only a year or so, we started having a multitude of problems. When my thoughts turned to moving to Portland, it shouldn't have surprised me that her immediate response was, "No."

Who could blame her? She was a big fish in a little pond. She had three young kids and a soon-to-be ex-husband who certainly didn't make anything easier, not to mention the difficulty of moving her family to Portland. She herself had been born and raised in Eugene so I'm sure even the idea of moving to a bigger city was a little intimidating, even without all the other complications. Oh, and did I mention she had also just come out. I mean like she was "new gay".

Prior to her coming out, if you had looked up "upstanding, cisgender, straight female," Jennifer's face would have popped up. It was a bit shocking to everyone, including me, when she *did* come out. But shit, how many people have ended up in straight marriages because being openly gay was terrifying, or possibly dangerous?

I'll never forget the moment I realized she was gay. We were sitting in the conference room, laughing about some lesbian thing I brought up. It was her pause that gave it away. The flow of banter back and forth halted for just a moment too long. Long enough for me to notice I was the only one still laughing. Something was off. I looked up from my papers, saw her blushing face and whispered out loud, "Oh my God. You're gay."

I had been completely out of the closet for a few years and had forgotten how ugly homophobia can be up close. It's not as if I was unaware of how continuously grueling it could be, but there's something especially heartbreaking when it comes from family and friends. The enormity of homophobia she faced when leaving her husband to be with a woman (cue, me) was unimaginable.

She was a locally grown, good Catholic girl from a well-known family, and an upstanding business and community leader. The picture perfect, all-American good girl. To say there wouldn't be a big celebratory coming out party for her was an understatement. Some of her "friends" openly criticized her, some gossiped behind her back, others completely ostracized her. Many people thought I had somehow turned her into a lesbian. Oh, how I've always wished I had that superpower! Any woman I wanted, all I'd have to do is look at her and say, "Look into my *eyes*. You are no longer straight—you are attracted to women." And by women, I mean me.

Her parents were devout Catholics. They attended Mass multiple times a week and put ash on their foreheads on Ash Wednesday. They were honest, kind, and sweet but definitely carried around the Father, Son and Holy Spirit. When it came to "homosexuality" they were of the mindset, "Love the sinner. Hate the sin." At one point in the office, prior to her coming out, Jennifer's dad Mike said he thought their son and I would make a great couple. Their *son*. A fellow office worker laughed and said, "Um, maybe you haven't noticed but Shaley bats for the other team," and we all laughed. Internally I was thinking, *Funny, because I'm really diggin' your daughter, Mike.*

For Jennifer, it was a nightmare. No matter what she did, there was no winning. Having three kids made things even more complicated, along with an ex-husband who knew all the right Catholic-guilt buttons to push to keep her in line. If all that wasn't enough, her career, which had been extraordinarily successful and a source of pride, started to tank. The pressure of it all, including pressure from me to move to Portland, was too much. Her response still hurt, but I understood. That was the final nail in the coffin for us. For me, there was no way in hell I could stomach living in a small town anymore. So, in the end, I moved back to Portland alone, while Jennifer stayed behind to rebuild her world without me.

As soon as I moved back, I bought a few houses and began selling real estate. I had all sorts of epic plans to buy and flip properties and seemed to be in a constant state of euphoria. Of course, I might have been euphoric from literally being high so often. No matter if I was elated naturally or not—what's that saying? "If you want to make God laugh, tell him your plans." Well, God was about to have one hell of a laugh.

By the time I'd moved back to Portland, when I miraculously and abruptly stopped drinking, I had 10 years of sobriety. Well, sobriety from alcohol. Unfortunately, I did not understand that addiction is addiction, is addiction, is addiction. You might be able to stop using one drug, but unless you understand the nature of the disease and, ultimately deal with the deeper issues, it's only a matter of time before a new addiction takes its place. It could be an actual drug, or it could be an addiction like shopping, work, or gambling. Really there are a plethora of "drugs" we use to numb ourselves. My drug of choice unfortunately, was one that could kill me.

I was unaware how deep and complicated my problems ran. Being closeted in this culture had definitely been a huge part of my pain. Unbeknownst to me at the time, the intense darkness I thought I had overcome in Idaho had simply gone dormant. There had been hints of something very troubling that popped up every once in a while, but it was easily dismissed and trivialized. Plus, there was always the option of taking a pill to suppress and obscure everything. *What's that? Oh, you're feeling unworthy and depressed, like you're being consumed by a never ending, confusing, black hole of emptiness? Well, take this pill and just keep pushing that shit way down deep, honey. I'm sure it'll go away.*

Even when I had a loving partner and close friends, those feelings of intense loneliness often consumed me. Subconsciously, I knew something awful still lurked inside, but I was too terrified to acknowledge it, let alone deal with it. One of my favorite sayings has always been "ignorance is bliss." On some level I've always envied people who could walk through life with blindfolds on, oblivious to the world around them. Instead of worrying, they'd hand over any personal responsibility to some God that, "knows what he's doing, so let's just accept it." I call bullshit. But then again, who am I to judge? With the amount of drugs I was consuming, I too was working hard to pretend everything was fine. I feigned attempts at convincing everyone my life was grand. But the continental divide between reality and my delusional life was growing. The last thing I wanted to do was acknowledge to myself, or anyone around me, that my insidious deeper issues were surfacing again.

As much as I longed for that blissful state of ignorance, I was unable to completely ignore and pretend my issues didn't exist— no matter how many pills I popped. My baggage remained intact. The drugs I did, in my feeble attempt to run away, only accentuated my struggles and deepened my ever-growing hole. How I wish I could have floated through the world, ignoring it all, without consequences. Oh wait, I did float through life high on pills—the crucial concept I kept missing was "consequences."

FOURTEEN
ROAD TRIP TO REHAB

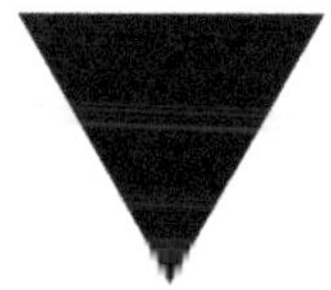

As I made the long monotonous drive back to Portland, my mind was a whirlwind of thoughts. *"What are you going to do in Portland? Can I really make it in real estate up here? Will I find a partner in Portland?"* My body tingled with the anticipation of new beginnings and possibilities. But then a wave of doubt and fear from the unknown would take over and leave my stomach, and of course intestines, unpleasantly gurgling. In the passenger seat sat my addiction who kept badgering me and offering pills to, you know, *relax*. Yes, my drug pushing pal tagged along posing as a friend, encouraging me to, "lighten up and take one" while also incessantly asking, "Are we there yet?"

It's hard to determine exactly when I went from controlling the drugs to the drugs controlling me. It was such a slow escalation, almost imperceptible until it was too late. One minute I was filled with contentment and joy, still able to function fully under the illusion of control. The next I was completely at the mercy of the drug, begging to be set free—or begging for more drugs. Not long after my surgery and being deluged by a seemingly never-ending supply of pills, my daily habit had actually died down slightly, to a sort of weekly party. A solo weekly party, as pill popping isn't typically a group drug activity.

The thing about pill addiction is most of the time it's easier to hide than alcoholism. Sure, you may slur your words a bit on painkillers, but it's nothing in comparison to being drunk. It also takes longer for you and others to realize the gravity of your situation and the depth of your addiction. When I started waking up with my night-shirt soaking wet, my joints aching, shivering from cold sweats, a certain panic crept in. *This can't be happening. I'm not a fucking junkie. This only happens to other people.*

We talk openly about addiction or alcoholism now. But during the '80's and '90's, no one really discussed it. We all saw the devastation and fallout when it touched a friend or family member, but almost everyone seemed to turn a blind eye. Instead of addressing the problem head on, people would talk around it, "She's OK. She's just going through a rough spot." or "Oh, Bob? Yeah, he loves his drink. He was pretty drunk that night. But funny, right?"

Most people knew about interventions, but they didn't become mainstream until the early 2000's. And it was certainly never talked about in the LGBT community. Yet statistically the rates of drug and alcohol addiction within our community were and continue to be much higher than within straight communities. It's fairly obvious that so much of my alcoholism and addiction came from shame and my struggles with my sexual orientation. Hindsight's always wonderful.

The other part of the problem was many LGBT were still struggling to even come out and live open lives. Most people I knew, including yours truly, carried some level of trauma from living a lifetime in a homophobic culture. And even if we were out, there weren't a whole lot of positive options for socializing in our loosely connected LGBT community. We wanted to meet and socialize with other LGBT people but doing that openly in public never felt 100% safe. Nor fun if you're looking over your shoulder, more concerned about your surroundings instead of engaging with fellow queers. So, we went to bars. Our bars. They were the main way that we were able to find community, with people like us. And what goes hand in hand with bars? Alcohol.

There were of course lesbian potlucks. We lesbians love a good potluck. But alcohol was there too. So, we drank, and often too much. We drank to have fun. We drank to fit in. We drank to ignore any lingering trauma from a lifetime of being shunned, ridiculed and feeling less than. And inevitably, some of us became alcoholics.

Amy and I had a lesbian friend Lisa visiting from Idaho one summer. We had gone out dancing and drinking the night before, with me drinking water as by then I'd given up alcohol. When I went into the living room the next morning, Lisa was sitting on our couch, her face swollen and hands resting on her knees shaking. "Good morning," I said breaking her out of some sort of trance. "Oh morning," she replied with a tremor in her voice, then looked back down. "Are you OK?" I asked hesitantly. "Yeah, yeah. I'm just not feeling my best right now," she said with a slight chuckle, clearly attempting to hide any embarrassment.

This was a common response. Her pretending she's not an alcoholic and me pretending it's just one night of over-doing it. But no one wakes up with sweaty trembling hands and jaundice colored swollen skin unless they've been at it for a while. And I knew that. But I didn't know what to do so when she asked for a beer at 8 a.m. to "calm her nerves" I gave it to her. It wasn't uncommon for people in our community to have high rates of alcoholism.

Painkillers were still fairly easy to get, whether I was living in Eugene or Portland. Just like in the past, I'd go the ER pretending to be in excruciating pain. And without fail, 99% of the time, I'd walk out with a prescription for opioids. But there was a problem—well one of my *many* problems. My tolerance had been steadily and rapidly increasing since surgery and had become almost a daily problem. In order to reach the high I was craving, I needed more and more.

The emergency rooms and hospitals were beginning to catch on. This was back in the early 2000s, when the country was starting to wake up to the out-of-control opioid epidemic. Hospitals started communicating with one another, reporting drug seeking behavior and connecting the dots. For addicts like me, this meant expanding my search for drugs to outside of the Portland area.

That year, while celebrating Father's Day with family in Salem, I was so far gone in my obsession for a fix, all I could think about the entire visit was hitting up the local ER for drugs. It was far enough from Portland that my chances of scoring were high. I hadn't seen my family in a while, so they wanted to catch up, "How's work, Shaley? Any new love interests? Are you happy being back in Portland?"

The questions were rolling out, one after the other. I just kept lying, embellishing the truth, pretending my life was fantastic. I sat there with my plastic smile, knowing I couldn't let them suspect for one second it was falling apart. *I am Shaley Howard. I have a successful career,* I told myself. *I am respected and own multiple properties. Plus remember, I stopped drinking years ago all on my own. I've made it.* Meanwhile, those idealistic musings were drowned out by thoughts of how quickly I could leave to get drugs.

There I was, surrounded by a family that loved me. My father, who fought relentlessly to make sure we were a family, who gave me the only real example of unconditional love I'd ever known. My sisters, who always made me laugh—especially Laurie, my touchstone. Being with my family was the one place I should have wanted to stay. Yet all I wanted was to leave.

I sat there, pretending to listen, while my mind looped, rehearsing what I was going to do and say when I got to the Salem ER. I visualized parking in the hospital lot, exiting my car in dramatically slow movements, acting like I could barely walk. These were important details as you never knew who might be watching. I envisioned hobbling through the sliding doors, my face contorted, loudly whispering to the reception nurse, "I need….to see…" I would pause here, "a doctor. I…" Another dramatic pause, touching my lower back for emphasis,

"my back…."

Sitting there, oblivious to the conversation, I audibly giggled at my own twisted daydream. "And the award for best acting in an addiction drama goes to…Shaley Howard!" Then I suddenly snapped out of it and noticed everyone staring at me. My face blushed and smile vanished. The conversation around me was very somber, about a sick relative. I'm certain they all thought I was losing it. Which, let's face it, I was.

"What's wrong with you?" Laurie asked while we cleaned up dinner. "Nothing. I'm just tired," I snapped back with a sigh. And that part was true. I was tired.

When I finally did score a prescription, I wanted nothing more than to binge, isolate, and float away without a care in the world. All my problems—the stresses of bills and work, and the undercurrent of emotional pain that haunted me—magically disappeared within minutes. Then the side effects of cottonmouth and intestinal "clogging" that most people disliked, I had actually started to enjoy. *What the actual fuck, Shaley?* To my addict body and mind, it meant I had been successful in my quest for drugs. I reveled in the glorious, albeit dysfunctional and grotesque, sensations.

Following my binges, I would experience bouts of heavy depression mixed with self-condemnation. I had worked through years of self-hatred and internalized homophobia, only to be consumed with a different kind of self-loathing. All the lying about (and often stealing of) drugs, knowing I was out of control was too much. I would stay in bed for days, lying motionless, staring up at the ceiling, unable to get out of bed. And if the depressive repercussions weren't enough, it wasn't long before I started experiencing physical withdrawals. No amount of over-the-counter painkillers seemed to ease my aching joints and nausea.

My routine would eventually return to some degree of normality, and I'd carry on like I had not just checked out for a couple days. Unfortunately, the in-between "normal" periods became shorter until once again, the only thing that dominated my thoughts was the excitement of another fix. There is a psychological and physical thrill of the chase that is part of addiction. My body would literally start tingling with goosebumps as I started to plan out another drug hunt. Like holding your breath after a lightning strike, waiting in thrilling anticipation for the boom of inevitable thunder to follow.

Whenever I had thoughts that interrupted and contradicted my planning process, suggesting my drug seeking behavior was destructive, the addict voice in me would quickly rationalize everything, making it all seem appropriate and acceptable. I was still able to convince myself I didn't need pills; they were a reward. "OK finish painting your living room, and then you can go get drugs," or, "Just show these people a couple more houses today and then we'll go to the ER and score. Stop sweatin' it."

That inner voice silenced any and all conflicting thoughts, every time. Even my peanut gallery, those internal voices that had been my background noise my entire life. The dominant voice-characters were usually either the two old men sitting in the balcony from the 1970s *Muppet Show*, or my favorite, Samuel L. Jackson. Always with the wise cracks and, every once in a while, a bit of wisdom. But never without an opinion. The newer voice rationalizing my drug use though was different and dangerous. And seemingly separate from my peanut gallery personas. It intentionally persuaded and lied. It seemed otherworldly, like an uninvited intruder, defensive and aggressively attacking any opposing voice. But it was still just me. It was my addict voice, who slowly began to dominate every decision I made.

Most people wake up in the morning, excited for a hot cup of coffee, thinking about all the things that day holds for them. My first thought? *Where can I get pain killers?* Things I had previously found important and an integral part of my life—animals, hiking, socializing with friends and family—became impediments. "Ugh, they're always wanting to go do things," I remember thinking one time after a call. All I wanted to do was get high and veg out. Soon, friends' calls went unanswered. As did those of family checking in on me. "I'm fine. Yes, work is fine. I gotta go," I'd say as I abruptly ended the call.

My real estate career that I'd worked so hard on building began to tank, along with my fat income, spiraling into nothing. In Eugene, I had achieved a six-figure income within a year in real estate. Six figures! Of course, I was sober and actually worked, so that helped. In Portland, as pill seeking dominated my life, I ignored my business and watched in a detached, numb state as bills piled up. The pressing need for pills consumed everything. I forgot how to function like an adult, or I just didn't care anymore. The more things spun out of control, the more drugs I needed.

The first thing to go was my own house. "It's totally fine," I shared with Amy, trying to hide my deep shame, "I just got a little behind on payments, so I'll sell it and move into my rental property." Oh, the lies. It wasn't OK—I mean, it was for a few months. Then my drug situation escalated further, and I wasn't able to manage my mortgage on that property either.

Even in my hazy, quickly deteriorating state, I knew the world around me—my house, my job, my friends and family, my health, all of it—was slowly sinking into a self-destructive, self-sabotaging hole. Strangely, I was very conscious of the spiraling storm I was trapped in, stuck in some altered dreamlike state, watching in slow motion as everything crashed down around me. I felt paralyzed, unable to simply stop the madness. I cried in secret, begging for some way out. I knew I was falling apart but couldn't escape. I cried out to God and the universe, "Please, *please* help me! Let me out!" Each time promising this or that, in exchange for freedom from drugs.

It's so easy when you are not in the middle of a disaster, self-imposed or not, to see the way out. But when addicted to drugs, you are no longer the person you used to be. It's a very gray and confusing area that many people, including addicts, often do not understand. At a certain point, you're no longer talking to the person you'd known all your life. You're lucky if you still see glimpses of them. Ultimately, you're talking to the drug.

The friends and family that were still around knew something was wrong. They rarely saw me, and when they did, I was either short with them or overly talkative—a lovely side effect of narcotics was Chatty Cathy. Once when on the phone with my dad, asking for money of course, he asked me directly if I was doing drugs. "Drugs? No, absolutely not," I said with shocked faux surprise, "I'm just having a hard time with work right now. My doctor did prescribe anxiety medicine, but that's all. I swear." Lie after lie.

My mom and I had similar interactions, but she was never as forward. She knew I would steal her pain pills any chance I could, but never confronted me. Instead, she would say things out loud to no one in particular, "You know I *thought* I had more pills. I just don't understand what happened to them all." She knew I was taking her medicine. In response, I would act like an oblivious asshole. Then I'd abruptly leave, too addicted to admit anything and too full of shame to stay.

Hospitals and my mom's medicine cabinet weren't the only places I'd obtain drugs. Any person's house I was in, I'd immediately ask if I could use the bathroom and silently search through cabinets, often scoring a few pills. It was surprising how many people just kept Vicodin in their main bathroom cabinet. I guess at the time most people had no idea those happy little pills were such a hot commodity, and they had no reason not to trust me. No one knew how far I'd fallen, and the liar and thief I'd become. The idea of being caught was still part of the thrill but, more importantly by then, I needed the drug to cope.

The combination of not knowing the power of these drugs, nor understanding the disease of addiction, made it a particularly hard time for addicts. Most people were completely unaware of how addictive opioids were, and at the same time, thanks to lying, greedy pharmaceutical companies, the US was being flooded with them. Families and communities were beginning to feel the ripple effects as they learned addiction doesn't just affect the addict—it touches everyone involved.

I finally gave up the struggle to keep my properties, and sold them all before the inevitable foreclosure set in. Amy let me move into her downstairs basement apartment. Yes, after years of owning multiple properties, a successful career, coming out, creating meaningful friendships, and finding wonderful partners, I had lost it all and was now living in best friend's basement.

Even though I still had my family, Amy was the only true friend I had left. But even she had a breaking point. I had pushed our friendship to the brink, not only financially but also emotionally. "I'm so sad and lonely," I kept saying over and over. "I'm sorry," she said sympathetically, not knowing how to help. How could she, really? What was she supposed to do? From an outside perspective, with no extensive understanding of or experience with the disease of addiction, I'm sure I looked like I was wallowing in self-pity. Instead of actually doing something about my downward, spiraling life, I did nothing. Plus, Amy had never been the syrupy sweet type of person anyway.

There are two kinds of friends. There's the kind you go to when you need tender reassurance and sweet words, even if you know they're perhaps not entirely true. "Oh, honey, I am *so* sorry! You did nothing wrong. What a cruel world! You are a beautiful human being; don't you ever forget that!" Then there's the friend who tells you straight up what time it is and does not mince words. They're bold and get right to the point. Amy and I would joke often as she was definitely the latter. Her brand of reassurance was more like a friendly smile and a stern pat on the back. "There. There." Unsaid translation? "Buck up, babe. Life is hard sometimes." It was a sort of hard love.

Maybe she has a bit of British stiff upper lip in her, who knows. But I knew she loved me and genuinely cared. I think she, like everyone else, didn't know how to help me. I was my own train wreck heading full speed into the station, and given the time period and circumstances, there was nothing they could have done until I hit rock bottom.

It wasn't pretty. Each day became a hellish nightmare. My life finally came to the point where my only concern was getting my drug. I had been psychologically addicted for a while, with thoughts of drugs streaming into my consciousness morning, noon, and night. I woke up in the morning wondering where I would get pills, then become more frantic at night when I could see only a handful remaining. *Where can I score tomorrow. I need more. What if I can't find any?* Even after I would score, the calm and somewhat grounded feeling wouldn't last long before desperate thoughts of scarcity flooded me again.

Shortly after moving in, my "new" living situation turned into a squalid mess of complete disarray. I no longer went grocery shopping and rarely did laundry. You couldn't even see the floors, as mounds of worn clothing piled up. Whenever I did have to get up, I'd lean over the side of my bed and grab whatever was within arm's reach. Shirts and pants were stained with food and grime from previous days, and I won't even talk about my underwear situation. My entire apartment smelled like sour milk and musty mothballs. I didn't care. Surprisingly, however, living in this self-created pig pen, I did somehow manage to shower regularly.

The warm water eased the pain that had become almost unbearable, radiating constantly through my skin and joints.

Drugs were taking their toll on my body. My eyes had become lifeless and sallow, marked underneath with permanent dark bags. My skin was blotchy and riddled with acne since all I ever did was hole myself up inside, curled up on my bed with curtains drawn. The athletic, muscular body I'd always taken pride in—the body that had taken me so far in life through sports—was withering away. "Who are you?" I asked, looking at the stranger, reflected in my bathroom mirror. A gray gaunt figure silently stared back. I was a shell of the person I used to be. Eventually I just stopped looking in mirrors.

Between my conniving, stealing, and consumption of drugs, there was also a sort of mourning taking place. I could see the person I used to be vanishing into nothingness. A person who used to be the epitome of health, honesty, and integrity. I knew I had lost weight, but no matter whether I was hungry or not, food wasn't important. What dominated everything was making sure I had my pain pills, and now, because my body was fully physically addicted, I had to have them—literally. The irony isn't wasted on me. The painkillers I originally started taking for fun and authentic back pain, were the same ones I now *needed* for a more extreme, self-induced, withdrawal pain.

My tolerance for Vicodin was so high, there were times I consumed what might have been lethal amounts under normal circumstances, sometimes 20 to 25 pills per day. Even with the astronomical amount I was taking, the withdrawal in my body prevailed. Later, I would learn that one reason for this was that consistently taking painkillers had caused my body to decrease the natural endorphins it typically provided for pain. The artificial painkiller your body is receiving fools it into thinking it no longer needs to produce as much. So, without the aid of an outside opioid, I was shit out of luck. Until my body started to produce more natural painkillers, I felt all the pain. And trying to withdrawal from narcotics without outside help is the kind of agony I wouldn't wish upon anyone. All those times I pretended to be in excruciating pain, I had *no* idea what true pain felt like.

That December, a rare snow hit Portland and blanketed the ground everywhere. Outside my basement apartment window, I could hear people joyfully playing as they reveled in the beauty of it all. Inside, my heart was racing as I was having a full-on panic attack. I was out of pills and stuck, unable to drive. The withdrawals were coming and there was nothing I could do. I laid there, coiled in a fetal position, rocking back and forth, desperately trying to find a position that would ease my pain for even one minute. My sheets were soaked from my revolving fever, then chills, then fever. It was as if my skin was on fire, searing with pain one-minute, icy bone-chilling cold the next. I was sweltering in a blanket of sweat and then moments later freezing, shivering uncontrollably.

The fun didn't stop there. I swear there were spiders crawling all over me. I panicked, slapping and scratching my skin, desperate to flick them off. Dark, red, raw spots started appearing on my arms and legs from the constant scratching. Then there were my joints. Every single joint screamed, as if on fire. No matter how I tossed and turned, there was no running from the pain—that just kept throbbing and pulsating in waves.

As if all these other withdrawal tortures weren't enough, I was also hit with extreme nausea as my poor kidneys tried to process the poison I kept feeding them. My stomach and intestines were twisted and cramping so severely that I'd run to the bathroom ready to explode. I'd plead for something to come out, wanting to expel the monster from my body. The bathroom floor became my second bedroom sanctuary. I laid there, soothing my fevered skin on the cold tiles, praying to no one in particular, wishing for an end to my suffering.

Then I had an epiphany. A doped-up, mindfucked, addict kind of epiphany, but an epiphany just the same. I decided that since I was out of pills, with no way of getting more, and I was unable to escape the physical withdrawals—I would self-medicate with alcohol. It would numb my pain enough so that I could get through the withdrawals. In this ridiculous plan I still, *still* thought I'd be able to return back to my regular life when it was over. And it never dawned on me to simply ask for help. I couldn't. At least that's what I thought. Even though I'm fairly certain everyone could see I was a hot mess, I was full of shame and far too embarrassed to ask. I had lost all my properties, my career, friends, and my livelihood. I was perilously close to losing my life, but my fear of openly admitting I was an addict still outweighed everything else.

My head pounded and my body screamed with agony as I placed the bottles of beer and hard alcohol on the store counter, wanting nothing more than to crawl back to my bed. I was disheveled and unkempt, standing there in stained clothing that hung from my body, in desperate need of a bath. *Don't judge me!* I screamed inside. The man behind the counter stared almost in disbelief, then handed me my change. I couldn't even look up as I fumbled for my coins and slinked out, the bell from the door clanking behind me. Every step back to my apartment felt like I was moving in slow motion through thick, viscous mud instead of powder-fresh snow. Each step weighed down by the gravity of my situation and increasing fatigue. I didn't bother with a glass when I returned, just opened a bottle and drank.

I hadn't had a drop of alcohol for almost 10 years, but it all came back in an instant. That burning sensation as it slid down my throat, and the immediate warmth filling my belly. And then, it finally happened. The agonizing withdrawal pain subsided. So, I drank more…and more…and more. The next few days were a blur as I cycled through drinking and blacking out. I had, in effect, dealt with my opioid withdrawal pain by taking myself down yet another dark hole. Having not had alcohol for years, my tolerance was low, but I was drinking like it was just yesterday. On top of that, the Lorazepam I'd been prescribed for anxiety, mixed with the alcohol, sent me into oblivion. Apparently 10 out of 10 doctors discourage the combination of alcohol and Lorazepam as it can have "life threatening consequences."

Amy found me, face down in a puddle of my own drool, passed out on the basement apartment floor. "Shaley! Oh, for fuck's sake, Shaley, wake up!" she yelled. I have a vague memory of her slumping me into her truck and rushing me to the ER where, apparently, I told the admission nurse that Amy was the one off her rocker. "I am *not* an addict!" I insisted with my thick cottonmouth tongue as I nodded in and out of consciousness, still drunk, full of Lorazepam and the remnants of opioids. Funny they went with Amy's version of the story.

The next thing I knew, I was at my dad's house in Salem. I had been checked in to Serenity Lane Recovery Clinic in Eugene and a bed would be ready the next morning. As I sobered up, sleeping in the guest bedroom contemplating how lost and dark my life had become, a fear like I'd never known enveloped me. My petrified body tightened with shivers, as I slowly pulled the blankets tight.

FIFTEEN

A BIZARRE HOMECOMING

Entering Serenity Lane was a bizarre homecoming. Most of the people who worked there were former addicts, so the gentle care and kindness that surrounded everything was palpable. I sat quietly, sober enough to understand the gravity of my situation while still dazed by the surreal nature of it all. "Is she on any drugs right now? How long has it been since she took her last drug or drink? Has she been in drug rehabilitation prior to this?" The stream of monotone intake questions faded in and out. I was trying to focus but the entire process had a sort of *Alice in Wonderland* dreamlike state, with me unsure if I was Alice or the Mad Hatter?

Swirling around these strange weighty sensations, there was also an airy lightness. A sense of freedom I hadn't experienced in years. The cat was out of the bag. There were no more secrets. Everyone knew my life had spiraled into the toilet and I had hit rock bottom. The question of whether or not Shaley Howard was an addict had been answered. I was a 40-year-old woman checking in—correction, being *checked in*—to drug rehab.

I sat slumped next to Dad absent of any agency, like a deflated child called into the principal's office. I was overwhelmed by shame while also feeling an odd buoyancy. I'd spent almost 10 years slowly developing a serious drug problem, the last part living in absolute chaos, repeatedly begging to be released from the invisible chains of addiction. Suddenly there I was, freed from that hell. Yet glancing up at my dad and seeing his damp, red-rimmed eyes, I experienced another kind of hell. I'm not sure what's harder, the heart-breaking pain of hurting someone you love, or enduring real physical pain.

My dad was someone I always wanted to please. He was my hero and the person I trusted and loved the most. I watched him stoically read through paperwork trying to hide his broken heart, and I wanted to reach over but knew I was powerless. It was only when we were upstairs at the detox center that he cried openly. "It'll be OK, Dad," was all I could think of to say. I knew how hollow and meaningless my words were. Interesting the small things you notice in times of tragedy, like how soft and gentle his embrace was as we hugged goodbye. He was quietly crying as I was escorted to my room. I decided it was definitely *much* harder hurting someone you love.

If I hadn't been almost paralyzed by a myriad of fears, I might have been laughing at the ridiculously circular nature of it all. There I was in Eugene, Oregon, where I'd been years ago as a scared little freshman attending the University of Oregon. I was now back as a grown woman, but this time for rehab. The successes and accomplishments I'd achieved in my life: coming out of the closet, stopping my drinking, purchasing properties, traveling…all of it just vanished. I'd gone from scared teenager to a grown, capable adult, back to a confused and terrified child. I'd lost everything and was laying on a flimsy twin mattress in an old dorm that had been converted to a drug treatment center.

When admitted to any rehab center, even if you are through the physical withdrawal stage, it's mandatory that you stay in the detox unit for observation. According to the hospital in Portland,

I had come close to dying. Who knew that when trying to get off narcotics by self-medicating, mixing alcohol and Lorazepam could have you accidentally knocking on death's door? Oh, that's right, all doctors knew. It turns out when you try a "do it yourself" home remedy with that particular combination of drugs, there's also a high probability of seizures.

I laid in my bed, feeling frantic as desperate voices ran amok in the dark. I pulled the wool blanket up to my chin as anxiety consumed me. Noise. The was nothing but a stream of panic and noise washing over me. Then, something happened. A voice emerged. Yes, I know what you're thinking, the girl's *finally*, 100% lost it—but it wasn't like that. It wasn't a voice from above bellowing down in a "Moses on the Mountain" moment. It was a soft, reassuring voice from within. It's actually hard to say exactly where it came from, but it definitely wasn't me or my peanut gallery. And it didn't come from outside me. It wasn't audible, at least not in the normal sense. It was, well, just…there. It was an all-encompassing, matter-of-fact, *knowing* sort of voice. Laying there, immersed in my hazy fog of fear, it simply said, "Everything will be OK. Let go." That's it. No long explanation. No heavenly lights or angels surrounding me. Just the simple, reassuring message of, "Everything will all be OK. Let go."

I am fully aware that an addict who just hit rock bottom and landed in a rehab detox center may not carry much credibility. I even laughed imagining myself trying to explain this to others, "No, really! I swear I was not hallucinating! Why *yes*, yes, I know I've been heavily medicated recently but I really did hear a voice!" I was sober and fully lucid. I also decided that it didn't matter if people believed me or not. To this day I believe some thing, some spirit or universal being, or some sort of loving presence…. *something*, reached out to me. More importantly, as soon as I heard those words, my fear melted away. One minute I was laying there petrified and the next I was flooded with a calm sense of inner peace. My body simply—and suddenly—relaxed. Like when you wrap a warm soft blanket, fresh out of the drier, around you. I knew instantly that no matter what happened, I would be OK.

For anyone thinking rehab is a place where you sit around giving each other warm fuzzies and sing kumbaya, I'm here to tell you: hell no. We did talk about our feelings often, but from 6:00a.m. until 9:00p.m. it was back-to-back scheduled activities and meetings. Once I was out of detox it was nonstop group and individual counseling sessions plus all sorts of Alcoholics Anonymous meetings. I learned everything there was to know about Bill, the founder of AA, and the "Big Blue Book." Or as people in rehab called it, my newly acquired "bible." I also had to memorize the Serenity Prayer, which was not very challenging as it was repeated in every AA meeting. There's no pretending in rehab. You can't just mouth the words like in church, trying to get away with lip-syncing hymns while having no clue what the actual words are. People knew. It was rehab. They always knew.

We talked about our feeling's ad nauseam. I am an extrovert and don't mind attention, but even I was tired of hearing myself talk. It was good to become so deeply connected and aware of my emotions, but I'd never talked about my feelings so much. It was exhausting! We'd sit around in a circle and people would share their "war stories," the horror of what they'd experienced prior to rehab.

I'd often sit there thinking to myself, *Good God! That's fucking unreal—and also pales in comparison to my story!* I'd then start contemplating how I would embellish my story to make it more salacious. My story was already—no doubt—fucking painful and hard, but some of the other ones…holy shit. "I know you got arrested three times, were sexually assaulted and beaten in prison, but wanna know what I did?" I know, ridiculous. There was an unbelievable pressure to constantly share in group.

No matter what I shared, though, there seemed to be a skeptical counselor who assumed I was withholding some major monumental lifetime trauma. One time, after vomiting up a mountain of emotional baggage, the counselor sat there staring in awkward, strained silence, while the rest of the group looked on empathetically. Then in a monotone, parental voice he quietly said, "Shaley, I just feel like there's more. Like you're holding back." I stared at him in disbelief thinking, *For fuck's sake, given my circumstances I'm pretty sure I'm not holding anything back.* What would be the point? I was one of the rare people, it seemed, who sorely wanted to be there.

The problem, I soon discovered, is that a lot of drug treatment facilities have what I refer to as the "lowest common denominator mentality." There's a huge intake of addicts, many of whom relapse within a week of finishing the program. In order to better manage everyone and have a higher success rate overall, they've had to develop a boilerplate, dumb-it-down approach. Even though each person is different in their recovery process, it's generally safer to assume everyone was starting at a low level of development and self-awareness. I also think many rehab facilities simply don't have enough resources or qualified staff to offer heavy doses of one-on-one attention. So at least for me, it was a simplified, bone-headed strategy that put us all in the same category.

One of the first things I heard in class was that 7 out of 10 residents' relapse within the first month. I audibly laughed, assuming it was some sort of scare tactic until I realized the instructor wasn't laughing. I was ignorant when it came to the disease of addiction, and very confused. Why would anyone, after going through even half of the hell I'd been through, decide to take drugs again? The last thing on the planet I ever wanted to do was return to that nightmare. The statistic was true, though. I was one of the luckier ones. I had years of sobriety between my use of alcohol and pills, which allowed for mental and physical growth. I also had a strong support network of family and friends (well *a* friend at least) which are key ingredients for sustained sobriety.

In the middle of my rebab experience, my sisters Laurie and Larisa came to visit a few times. They both lived in Eugene, so it was also easier than my other sisters who lived hours away. When my mom called to let me know she was coming to visit, my stomach dropped, and I suddenly felt anxious. Watching her walk through the main entrance and check-in at the front desk, I could feel my heart-beat ramp up, as if preparing for battle. Her eyes brightened when she saw me and she hurried over, embracing me in one of her mom bear hugs. I wanted to melt into her arms forever right then. Even with all the mixed messages I'd gotten use to over the years, her hugs still made me feel safe. For a brief moment I felt hopeful. Maybe this was it. This would be the moment I could have a heart to heart, honest conversation. One where I would finally be heard and understood.

Laurie and I took her on a tour. I kept giggling inside, realizing how strange and surreal it was I the tour guide for my mother at my drug rehabilitation center. "Now over on the left you'll see the cafeteria that has a buffet of healthy foods available almost any time of day. But no coffee. They view caffeine as a drug. OK, let's move on to the women's dormitory. And we're walking...walking...walking..."

After she'd taken in the place, we decided to get lunch in the cafeteria. That's when Mom started in about the cost of the facility and Chuck paying for it. "The money he spent on this," she grumbled, adding, "It should have been my money." I glance up at Laurie who was already rolling her eyes. I guess I should have been shocked but I wasn't. I looked back over at Mom and shook my head. There I was after losing everything in my life, including almost losing my actual life, sitting in drug rehab at the age of 40, and my mom was more focused on how my dad somehow jilted her 35 years ago.

Suddenly I was flushed with anger. I had taken drugs, yes to help me cope with being closeted, but they came in pretty handy when having to deal with Mom over the years too. I was trying so hard to deal with my train wreck of a life completely sober, no longer able to take the drugs that had provided such a nice buffer between me and her. Laurie saw my face redden and reached under the table and put her hand on my knee. She knew I was about to blow. Her simple touch grounded me and conveyed the message I needed to hear. *"I love you. Focus on you right now. This is not worth your precious energy while healing. This version of Mom will still be there when you get out."*

What was surprising about rehab was, in many ways, it was fun. Yes, oddly enough—fun. I certainly wouldn't have chosen to be there if I'd been in my right mind. I probably would have chosen to go to Six Flags, screaming with delight on roller-coaster rides. But I wasn't in my right mind and being in a place surrounded by people who had experienced similar hells was like finding another family. Who knew I had a whole other dysfunctional family waiting for me at Serenity Lane?

Drug rehabilitation was full of laughter. Belly-aching, tears of joy laughter. There was a certain freedom and safety that emerged from releasing all your secrets while surrounded by people who've struggled as hard as you. Drug addiction in this culture carries such a harsh and negative stigma. Addicts are seen as lazy, disgusting, and weak—pariahs of our society. An addict's life is one of pain and isolation. Being surrounded by other people who shared similar paths helped to alleviate the planetary weight of loneliness, dejection, and marginalization we'd experienced for years. There was a universal and immediate understanding, a nod almost, that made it unnecessary to constantly unpack the sordid, intimate details of our addict life. A bunch of humans who'd bottled up everything, we were finally beginning to release a torrent of emotions that, fortunately, included levity and laughter. It also reminded us of what it could feel like to be alive and human without drugs. None of us felt so dreadfully alone anymore.

Many of us were capable, high functioning adults that were predisposed to the disease of addiction. We wanted to be free of it but couldn't or didn't know how. So, while we tried to stifle our emotions and problems with drugs, addiction kept knocking on the door, interrupting.

Part of our daily recovery schedule was some sort of physical workout regimen. What we decided to do in that time was up to us, but it was a mandatory part of the program. Every morning at 6:00a.m., a group of us would head down to the local YMCA to start trying to rebuild our withered, drugged-out bodies. But any time we left the premises of Serenity Lane, we were required to have a counselor accompany us. As a grown adult it was incredibly embarrassing to have a chaperone. Clearly, however, we had not made the best choices in life up to that point, so perhaps it was a good idea to have "Mom" or "Dad" tag along.

Usually, counselor Barbara joined in that early morning fun. She too was a former addict, which made her relatable and trustworthy. She'd pepper us with questions about our lives as we walked, genuinely interested. Barbara had a nonchalant, laid-back disposition that was infectious, and almost made it seem like a large group of grown adults walking down a dark street at 6:00a.m. wasn't weird. Almost.

I appreciated the light-hearted way she showed up, because behind my fun-loving appearance, I still carried enormous amounts of shame and embarrassment. As a grown woman, having to ask permission was humbling. "Shakin' the bush here, boss!" as Paul Newman would say in *Cool Hand Luke*. Yet the entire experience continued to feel so surreal, what else could I do but put on a brave face and laugh?

Once inside, we'd gravitate to whichever workout area suited us. My new rehab buddy Sue and I would head over to the weight-lifting area. It's interesting the friendships that develop in drug rehabilitation centers. Sue was born and raised in a small town in Southern Oregon. She was a mother of three kids, never attended college and—besides rehab—had only traveled close to home. In another life, we likely wouldn't have even developed an acquaintanceship. She talked about her kids, reminisced about high school boyfriends and how she met her husband. Then there was me—a lesbian who loved sports, my dog, politics, and nature.

When you strip away all the superficial differences, however, a strange unifying process emerges. Ultimately, all those man-made boundaries we're taught to categorize people only end up dividing us: where you are from, how much money you make, the color of your skin, your education, your sexual orientation, your gender identity, your marital status. Underneath all those layers, there were simply two human beings that found an abundance of overlapping commonalities.

In rehab, all façades are dropped, whether you want to give them up them or not. Even though some of the topics we shared weren't necessarily mutual interests, when we stopped hiding in society's hierarchical, fabricated cliques, we saw a real person. Drug addiction is a great equalizer. There's nothing like stripping away everything you thought you were and taking away the things you thought you had.

Watching my skinny new friend struggle to lift an obscene amount of weight, I casually suggested she try lifting something that wasn't the mass of an elephant. She dismissed my advice and kept squirming and grunting to no avail. It was entertaining but ridiculous. "I can't! I can't do it!" she finally blurted out, throwing the weights down, a loud *clang* ringing as they bounced off the rubber mats. Staring at her while giggling and confused as to why she was lifting so much in the first place, I realized she was genuinely upset.

Maybe it was the pressure of drug addiction and rehab and feeling completely out of control. Whatever her personal reasons, I understood and empathized with her frustration. I walked up to her, put my hands on her shoulders, looked directly in her eyes and with a deadpan voice said, "Hey, no one likes a quitter. Well, except in rehab. Then it's OK." There was a moment of silence before we both began to laugh. Laughter always helped. It was the salve that eased our pain.

Even though I was completely clean of drugs a week into my rehab experience, my journey was just beginning. Yes, there was laughter, but pain continued to loom. When my drug-induced haze started to lift, the clarity and extent of my train wreck was dreadfully obvious. Not only were my personal accomplishments and successes in the garbage, but I had also left a litany of people hurting and confused in my wake. It's a conundrum of sorts. One of the main reasons people continue using drugs is actually because we don't want to face the extent of the chaos we've created from using drugs in the first place. So, you keep using to escape the reality of what your life has become, which only continues the cycle of destruction.

I knew when I walked into the main meeting room that morning, I was doomed. The notoriously uncomfortable metal folding chairs that accompany every AA meeting were arranged in a large circle, filling the room. In front of every other chair was a carton of Kleenex. My peanut gallery immediately jumped into action, *Nope. Turn around and go back.* But of course, I didn't run away. I steeled myself, straightened my shoulders, and found a chair next to Dad, Geri, and Laurie.

One of the more effective—while simultaneously awful—activities held at Serenity Lane were family group meetings. Much of the recovery process involves making amends, so it was important for addicts to face the people we'd hurt. Everyone in the room had one person joining them. I on the other hand, had three people. I couldn't tell if I was incredibly lucky or unlucky. In hindsight, I've decided I was the luckiest person in that room. But holy hell, let the games begin.

Each person was supposed to write a letter about their experiences. One from the addict to a family member and one from the family member to the addict. They were brutal. Talk about facing the music. I watched as both the addict and their family member read their letters aloud, in front of each other and the entire group. Each one described the horrors they'd been through, and their emotional roller coaster ride. Tissues were pulled left and right from the Kleenex box.

Then it was my turn. I turned and faced Laurie, Dad, and Geri. I could feel the sweat beading up on my face and arms. I'd been clutching my letter so tightly that my handwritten words had started to smudge. With a shaky voice I read, "I want you all to know, I'm very sorry. I wish I had come clean and told someone about my problem. I know I lied to you all." It went on in this vein for another few paragraphs. It was all I could think of to write the night before, "I'm sorry." There was nothing I could do or say to convince anyone I was trustworthy. "I give you my word," meant nothing anymore. So, I apologized. Over and over.

Then it was time for my family to read. During my apology letter, Laurie and Geri had already started in on the Kleenex. I kept telling myself to keep it together. I didn't want to break down in front of everyone. I already felt like I'd been turned inside out for the world to see every ounce of my ugly. I needed just one tiny morsel of mercy. Geri proceeded through her moist eyes, to tell me how much she loved me in great detail. She ended with a heartbreaking, "I just can't trust you right now." Knowing I had to face what I had done and how deeply my addiction had affected others, I kept eye contact—until that part. She looked up with tears streaming down her face and I couldn't bear anymore. My heart sunk and eyes fell to the ground in shame.

After a few moments, Laurie proceeded to read her letter. Trying to hold back my tears, I emitted an awkward, nervous laugh. She reached out and touched my knee, letting me know without words that she loved me. Her letter was entirely about how she missed her sister, how much she longed to be able to call me up again and share everyday, mundane stories that only we would find humorous. She said she couldn't imagine a world without me and ended her letter with how she missed "Shaley the Great." This was how I always signed cards to my family. It was my way of joking around, and had started when I was just a kid, jumping off the couch, wearing a towel wrapped around my shoulders like a cape, as I shouted, "Look out below! I'm 'Shaley the Great!'"

I could feel my salty tears welling up after she finished. Trying desperately to hold them back was an absurd exercise in futility—yet there I was again, trying to mask my pain. Defensively, my sarcastic and protective peanut gallery chimed in, *What the actual fuck? Why doesn't anyone else have to endure three letters? This is so unfair.* They were quickly dismissed as I remembered my dad asking me at an early age, "Who told you life is fair, Shaley?"

My attention shifted back to the room as my dad cleared his throat and began his letter. Honestly, I don't remember much of what he read. His disposition was once again stoic, almost as if he were giving a college lecture. It wasn't his words I heard, but the palpable pain beneath them. There was such great love mixed with incredible sorrow. I do remember him looking up with glossy eyes, finishing with the same, "I also miss Shaley the Great."

Those last words, combined with the heartbreaking weight of Geri and Laurie's letters, were too much. I broke down and let the tears fall. *Goddamnit!* I didn't care anymore about my pride, or anyone seeing me collapse. I had hit rock bottom and hurt so many people. People I cared about and loved. We all sat there dabbing our eyes with Kleenex while everyone else watched. It was a step. Perhaps just a small step towards healing, but a step nonetheless.

As we were saying our goodbyes, a sick, rotting feeling gnawed at me. It was like a ball of tightly wound rubber bands made entirely of anxiety and fear, ready to snap. Everything constricted and I was suddenly petrified. Of what, I didn't know. You'd think after experiencing such a cathartic moment of love and connection, I would've been elated and relieved. But I was flooded with a strange, crushing fear. Perhaps because in reality, it hadn't been a small step at all. In actuality, it'd been a terrifying, monumental leap towards rebuilding and healing broken relationships. Not to mention healing Shaley Howard

As that anxiety washed over me, I frantically thought, *What do I do now? Will they ever trust me? What if I screw up…then what? I'll have no one.* As if on cue, Geri, the last one to leave, leaned over and whispered, "You are stronger than you think you are, honey," and then walked out. Hearing those words of confidence helped me more than Geri would ever know. At a time when I couldn't see my own strength, my own worth, someone else did. She reminded me I was much stronger than I thought I was. For that, I was and am forever grateful.

Ever since the "voice" told me everything would be OK, something had shifted. I guess a lot had shifted. Like those pictures within pictures I would see in books. You know the ones where if you stare long enough, or squint your eyes, or try not to focus…. eventually something in your vision shifts and another image appears. I would always flip to the back of the book to find the answer. Then it would be obvious and easy to spot. Without cheating, I was never able to see the tiger, or cow, or whatever cool alter-image was hiding in plain sight.

That shift in perspective happened that first night laying on that dorm room bed. As if something nudged me and woke me up, a veil was lifted by those simple words, "Everything will be alright. Let go." Things seemed somehow clearer. It was like having a religious experience completely absent of any religious dogma.

From that moment on, things that seemed previously significant and meaningful felt almost trivial. Making a huge income or being number one in my business didn't seem as important.

It wasn't that I lacked the desire for money or material things, it was that relationships and community had become more meaningful. For years, I had been concentrating on money and status, and now that aspect of my life seemed rather hollow. Much like a child letting go of its favorite toy, I'd moved on to something more captivating and fulfilling. Maybe I'd pushed myself through another level of spiritual evolution, or maybe something pushed me towards it. Who knows? In any case, it all seemed so *obvious*. How had I not seen it so clearly before? The picture within the picture is always apparent after you see it.

I had been in rehab for 21 days when the counselors decided to release me early. Most people stay around 28 days. I had made significant progress and had a strong support system, which was critical to staying clean and not relapsing. When I spoke with the counselors about early release, my first thought was, *I win!* Then I laughed at how obnoxiously ridiculous and competitive that sounded. *It's not a contest, Shaley. If it were, no one would want to enter this contest. Take it down a notch.*

Then reality hit. I was heading home to a complete disaster. Cue gut wrenching nausea and anxiety. I had successfully gotten off the insane roller coaster ride of drugs, thanks to my family and counselors, but there was still a world of grief just waiting for my return.

SIXTEEN

WELCOME BACK

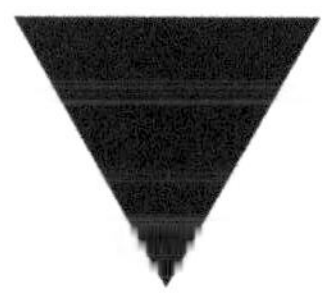

We walked into my apartment and the smell of musty unwashed clothing and rotting food almost knocked us over. By the foul, repugnant stench, I was certain something had died and its decaying carcass was buried in the piles of junk. Based on Dad and Geri's expressionless faces, it was hard to tell what they were thinking. They looked exhausted though, like they'd both aged ten years over the last 21 days. *I bet you are super happy you had kids right about now!* I thought making sure I didn't audibly laugh at my self-indulgent humor. They, I'm certain, were not finding anything funny about my situation. But humor and laughter were keeping me afloat and my fear and embarrassment at bay.

"I love you both," I'd said on the ride home, "but I don't want any help cleaning up my mess." I wasn't sure if they would have offered but I wanted it off the table. After walking in and seeing my massive chaotic space, I momentarily thought perhaps I had been a little too eager pushing their help away. But it was my train wreck and I needed to clean it up myself. After hugging goodbye, I turned and slowly began wading through my mess, thinking, *Ugh. Now where did I put my apartment floor?*

The state of my finances was beyond a train wreck. I had racked up so many "medical" bills from seeking drugs, along with other miscellaneous expenses, to say I was in the red wasn't even close. It was more like screaming, five-alarm, hot-pepper red. Even though I knew I'd never be homeless, thanks to my family's support, the stress of possible financial ruin was gut wrenching. Oh wait, I *was* in financial ruin. I had no income, no properties or anything of value, and no feasible way to repay anything yet. The cherry on top was the never-ending fucking bill collector calls threatening to take everything I had. "Um…OK. Come get it," was my usual response. Seriously, at that point there was nothing left to take.

I had been dreading cleaning up my train-wreck, but especially my finances. I knew how alarming my situation had become. Luckily, Dad and Geri continued their support. I mean, come on—they weren't going to abruptly stop helping me after I just got out. They'd just paid for a very expensive rehab, so it would've been shocking if at such a pivotal turning point, right when I was clean and sober, they cut me off. And in order to get back up on my feet, I desperately needed to have a buffer for a few months so I could start piecing my life back together. It wasn't much but enough money for the basics; food, rent, gas money etc. If there was ever a time in my life I needed that help, it was then.

It quickly became clear that the best solution to make my way back to some sort of financial stability, was to declare bankruptcy. For those out there who've never experienced bankruptcy or shitty credit, I'm here to tell you it is extraordinarily confusing while simultaneously mortifying. I thought being an addict and lesbian was challenging, but holy shit, try adding bad credit and bankruptcy. It's another societal taboo no one wants to discuss. The judgement I faced was immediate and surreal.

Back when I sold real estate, I occasionally came across people struggling with credit. It never dawned on me to pass judgment, though. I never knew what people's circumstances were and figured they were doing the best they could with what they had. Don't get me wrong, I'm no angel and I've definitely had my share of self-absorbed, holier-than-thou moments of judgement. But in this area for some reason, it always felt like a bridge too far. Suddenly, I was part of the crap credit and bankruptcy club, barely able to make ends meet. It's nerve-racking standing in line at the grocery store, waiting for your turn, wondering if your prepaid card would work. Yes, I was nervous about a *prepaid* card! Most of the time I would have enough money, but occasionally my card would be declined. I'd see disapproving looks out of the corner of my eye and sometimes literally hear people "tsk"ing" me. Not everyone, but there was usually one. I'd walk out of the store empty handed and sit in my beat-up Honda and sob. "What the fuck do you want from me?" I'd shout out to the always-silent ether, "Fucking tell me, because I'm trying to do the right thing. I know you can help me but clearly you don't want to. You are the creator of *All*, but apparently can't manage one simple conversation with me?" This would go on for a while, me screaming as many derogatory epithets as I could think of into the air. During these tragic meaning-of-life monologues I did, however, hear from my peanut gallery. Always chiming in with a bit of levity, "Young lady, there will be no existential discussions on your life's purpose until you can address the creator of the universe in a more calm and polite manner." The blasphemy of it all. Eventually I'd tire, my tears would dry, and I'd head home. No matter how depressing my situation felt, however, it seemed my damn optimism eventually won out. The glass was always half full. Barely half full, but half full nonetheless. I'd always been a somewhat positive person overall, but during that time period my optimism was exceedingly high. Why you may ask, given that my life at that moment was completely in the crapper? The "pink cloud." This is a phenomenon that happens to people after being released from rehab. The addict experiences feelings of euphoria from being sober and clear-headed after years of using. Geri likened it to the natural high prisoners feel when joyfully falling and kissing the ground following years of incarceration.

And woah, was I riding this cloud. Yeah, baby! I was sober and had a new life! Every day was a new beginning, and I would constantly, and oh-so-annoyingly, let everyone know. I was like Mary-fuckin'-Poppins on crack with my perpetually cheery disposition. OK, maybe not the best analogy, but you get it. More importantly, aside from being continually and nauseatingly positive with everyone, the pink cloud gave me the extra boost of energy I needed to endure the cleanup phase of my drug aftermath.

Prior to this particular life implosion, I had somehow managed to set up the essential operational paperwork for my pet care business. I have no recollection as to how I managed to do this, but everything was in order. I just needed clients. So, I decided with a little help from my magical pink cloud dust to do what I did best: sales. I went door to door with my business card and brochures. I had no money for advertisements, and there was no way in hell I was going to ask my dad for money. I mean good Lord; he'd just spent thousands on my rehab. So, I walked. And walked. And then I walked some more. Every single day, I would knock on doors, introduce myself politely, and ask if they needed help with their dogs or cats.

One chilly, drizzly afternoon, I was diligently out knocking when a deep fatigue gripped me. I'd been walking and knocking for hours with zero luck. In fact, up to that point, even with weeks of handing out my brochures, I still had not attained one client. I knew in my gut my idea would work if I just could catch a break. I'd had years of experience running my own business, plus I was passionate about animals. I just needed a chance.

But it was impossible to ignore my overwhelming sense of hopelessness that day. My clothes were soaked through from the rain, I was shivering, and my feet were throbbing. My pink cloud had turned a depressing shade of gray. I began to tear up as the weight of everything flooded me. I just stopped, right there in the middle of the sidewalk, with rain splashing all around me. I stood there motionless, staring ahead aimlessly, full of doubt and despair.

Then some of the positive messages from rehab flashed before me. The awakening that happened to me there. That feeling of living in fog for years, always fumbling for direction, then suddenly being offered the gift of clarity and peace. Not only a way out but another way of living, like sunlight piercing through the clouds and illuminating pathways I'd never seen before. Yes, it's hard not to sound corny when describing such things, but they felt real and almost otherworldly. I'd been given a second lease on life with a new vision and different priorities.

Standing there soaked to the bone, remembering those messages, I decided to mentally try letting go. "It'll all work out, Shaley. Have faith," I earnestly whispered. Then, and I am not shitting you, within only a few moments, everything in my disposition shifted. The heaviness I'd unknowingly been carrying in my body vanished and I was left with a serene sense of levity and peace. I stopped crying and continued walking and knocking with a new, strange air of lightness. It was more than just a conscious understanding that worrying wouldn't help, it was a physical transformation. As if my cells were working in conjunction with my mind and had found a way to release all negative energy. Similar to, but on a far lesser scale, what I experienced my first night in rehab.

The funny thing is, once again, it all seemed so obvious. Like the answer of letting go and just being present was there all along yet somehow, I routinely missed it. Similar to when you're watching a horror flick and every single person has been hacked to pieces by some ax murderer, yet the lone survivor walks into the dark basement saying, "Hello? Is there anyone there?" You're screaming at the screen, "Get the fuck out!" The answer was so ridiculously obvious…don't go down into the basement, dummy.

The decision to let go was always right there in front of me. I could continue to move in the direction I wanted to go for work and rebuild my life, but at a certain point, much of what happened was out of my control. Have I mentioned addicts usually have issues with control? Ultimately, whatever was going to happen would happen, and there wasn't a damn thing I could do about it. *So, lighten the fuck up Shaley, enjoy the ride and let go.*

Right about then I felt my phone vibrate. Since at this point in my life I'd alienated most of my friends, I assumed it was a family member checking in on me. To my great surprise, it was someone inquiring about dog walking. My first client. As I hung up, all I could do was laugh. In that moment I not only realized but fully believed there was something to this message of "letting go." In rehab they called it, "Let go and let God." Whatever the source of it, I was bursting with appreciation and gratitude.

Life at that time seemed to offer up a never-ending supply of opportunities and lessons. Case in point, my first house sitting gig. It honestly never dawned on me that house sitting would be such a large part of my business. But as it turned out, people really like having someone actually stay with their pets. However, what I learned the hard way was to always check out the house before agreeing to house sit. Being a newbie to the pet care business (and eager for clients) I figured beggars can't be choosers.

The house was fairly far from my place and driving back and forth in my barely running car put a strain on my growing daily commitments. It also came with three large, rambunctious German Shepherds that ruled the roost. If that wasn't enough, this house could've easily been a contender for the show *Hoarders*. There were piles of laundry, old magazines, used dog toys—pretty much anything under the sun—cluttering every inch. It was gross. I mean, if *I* thought it was disgusting, it was disgusting. I was a junky that had lived in my own pigsty for over a year prior to rehab, so I was pretty much the expert on pigsties. I clearly wasn't one to judge others about cleanliness, but that didn't mean I wanted to go back to living in filth, even temporarily. Yet since I'd already made the mistake of agreeing over the phone prior to seeing the place, it was important to me, especially after rehab, to keep my word. So, I stayed.

Turned out, one of the German Shepherd dogs, Maxine, had extreme hip problems. Those poor German Shepherds with their inherited hip dysplasia. What this meant for me was physically wrapping a harness around her abdomen and holding her up whenever she needed to walk, pee, or…well, you can guess the rest. When the owner was explaining dog care details, I stood there motionless, mouth agape. She asked me if I was OK. I was stunned into unmovable silence thinking, *Every single time she needs to go to the bathroom, I have to pick her up—this 75-pound dog—and hold her stationary while she does her business in the yard*. Realizing I was staring ahead like a zombie, I regained my composure and reassuringly replied, "Oh no, I'm great! This…this is absolutely no problem," adding, "so how long are you going to be gone again?"

By far, the worst part of that first gig was poor Maxine required painkillers. And not just any painkiller—Vicodin. I couldn't fucking believe it. *Well hello, friend*, I thought as I was rolling the white pill around in my palm. Luckily, the aftermath of my addiction to pills was similar to my drinking. Once I had completely stopped and it was out of my system, something just clicked. The craving and desire to take them all but vanished.

However, I was also familiar with the sneaky way addiction works and decided to call it out. Literally. I grabbed the phone and dialed my dad, announcing, "Hey, I'm looking at pain pills right now that I need to give to this dog. I just wanted to let someone know." By publicly acknowledging the painkillers were in my presence, any possible control they had over me seemed to disappear.

Physical addiction is hell, but the psychological aspect of addiction is hell with Satan at the wheel, laughing maniacally while spinning 90 miles per hour donuts in the parking lot. That's the part that usually fucks people over and why relapsing is so common. It's not the physical part, it's your conniving mind twisting the truth and convincing you things will be better with one more hit.

I learned there was great power in shining a light on my addiction. By taking away its secretive nature, much of its psychological power faded. I'd spiraled down the rabbit hole for years, keeping my drug habit underground. But once I was able to detox and physically get clean, I realized the only true power addiction had over me was the power I gave it. As soon as there were no more secrets, worming their way in and out of my consciousness, the temptation and psychological pull slowly died out. Ultimately for me, once I was clean and out of rehab, it all came down to a choice.

This is a very gray area when talking about addiction. To refer to it as a "choice" can be confusing and misleading to many who are not familiar with the disease of addiction. It is all very complicated. Outsiders who have a limited understanding and who've been inundated with our culture's ignorant, negative stigmas attached to it, may think people are simply lazy or choosing to take drugs to get high and party. Perhaps *some* are in the beginning. And honestly, I'd be lying if I didn't admit, yeah, some drugs are fun. But drinking a beer, popping a pill, or smoking a joint occasionally is much different than becoming an addict. No one chooses to become an addict.

The physical and psychological aspects of addiction are multifaceted and never simple. Every addict experiences a different level of physical and psychological addiction. Each individual's progress and success in recovery is unique to them. I counted myself extremely fortunate that my experience with addiction, especially the recovery phase, was drastically different than many people I met. Once I was physically clean and given the information and tools to stay sober, my path to recovery soared.

My addict mind soon lost much of its power over me. But no matter how far along in my recovery I was, I couldn't forget that no matter what, I was and always would be an addict. It didn't mean I was using. It meant I had to remember it was part me and never fool myself into thinking my addiction vanished. The moment you believe it's gone is the moment it starts to sneak back in with insidious lies and rationalizations.

Following my completion of in-patient rehab, I was repeatedly told if I wanted to increase the odds of my long-term success, I should seek out an AA meeting right away and register for a weekly three-hour outpatient program. I immediately did both. There was no fucking way I was going back to that living hell. They told me to jump, I asked how high.

Since I was only familiar with the AA meetings from rehab, I didn't realize there were different types of group meetings to choose from, such as women's only groups, lesbian groups, gay and lesbian, and so on. As an ignorant newbie to the scene, I was fiercely determined to attend a meeting right away. So, I simply picked one that was close to my place. Walking in and seeing the group, I swear if I hadn't been riding my pink cloud, I would have run for the hills. I could feel my leg muscles tensely fighting me to turn back as I forced them down the stairs.

First, why are so many AA meetings located in dark, dank basements of churches? Second, what's with the cold, uncomfortable metal folding chairs? I understand not wanting cushy-chill lounge furniture as eventually you want people to leave. But after five minutes in those chairs, my butt was icy and numb, screaming and begging for relief.

The worst part of this meeting was it consisted entirely of older men who lived by the AA blue book—the "bible." Emphasis on *bible,* as to them, it might as well have been the actual bible.

Discovering I was fresh out of rehab, for two painful hours they preached to me about how to stay sober: what I needed to do, who I should talk with, and even what to do in my free time. I know they were trying to help but fuck me, talk about mansplaining. I guess cross talk was acceptable at this meeting. *Oh my God, this is my life now. I'm going to have to sit with these grouchy know-it-all men for the rest of my life in order to stay sober,* I thought. Then laughed thinking, *This might just make me want to use again.* But I sucked it up, stayed, and did the most important thing. I stood up and shakily said, "My name is Shaley and I'm an addict."

After the meeting, the intelligent part of my peanut gallery suggested that perhaps there were other meetings I could choose from, not just the one closest to my apartment. Brilliant! I ended up at the Wednesday night AA/NA meeting solely for women and lesbians. Lord have mercy, I found my people. It was full of lesbians! As I sat down next to a woman with a lifetime of experience etched in her face, I uttered out loud, "Thank *God*." She looked at me quizzically while I confessed that prior to finding this group, I seriously thought I was doing some sort of penance having to hang out weekly at the men's group. With kind eyes she smiled and said, "Well, you are safe here. At least from opinionated men. Lesbians wanting to 13th step you? Well, that might be another thing."

Not knowing what 13th stepping was, I curiously smiled but was clearly confused. I knew the 12 steps of recovery but apparently there was one I missed. A 13th step. Turns out, there isn't an actual 13th step to recovery. 13th stepping is when a person already experienced with the program seeks out newbies for romantic relationships. Once she explained this I laughed, "Well, if that's my biggest problem right now, I'll take it."

The women in this group were exceedingly welcoming and I was immediately at ease. There were a couple of women that seemed to want more than friendship, but overall, I felt at home. The only difficulty was sharing. I had no problem standing up and identifying myself as an addict. But fuck me, sharing more than name, rank, and number was the worst. I mean, I may not have wanted a new romantic relationship at that particular moment in my life, but I was still human. There were some hot lesbians in that room! When it came my turn to share my story and offer up the most embarrassing and degrading moments of my life, it was a bit challenging. I eventually got over myself, however, realizing that staying sober was far more important than my vanity. And contrary to my Aries nature, life wasn't always centered on me. *Reality check, babe.*

Those AA meetings, building up my business and outpatient weekly group sessions, were my life for a while. It seemed all I did was talk ad nauseum about my feelings and listen to people's tragic life stories. At some point, it became obvious my recovery process was different than a lot of others. When I stopped drinking years earlier, something just clicked. The same was true with pain killers.

Inevitably in these meetings, I ended up connecting with other addicts. That seemed natural, but over time, I began to question if drugs and alcohol weren't the cornerstone of our relationship, would we be friends? They were nice but often the only thing we seemed to have in common was addiction. Anytime I tried to broach the subject that perhaps for my personal journey, regular AA meetings had run their course, everyone told me I was in denial. "As soon as you tell yourself you don't need meetings, Shaley, you'll be heading towards using again."

Addicts are in a kind of funny "damned if you do, damned if you don't" situation. If you contradict drug counselors or other people in the program, it's assumed you're in denial. You can't win. So even though I was certain I wasn't in denial, it was challenging trying to convince the outpatient counselors I didn't need group sessions anymore. The moment I started trying to ease my way out, they doubled down.

"Shaley, I feel I've failed you," my outpatient counselor David stated. I sat there just staring back, unsure how to respond. Once I realized the conundrum I was in, and the apparent "no escape" clause, all I could do was laugh. I may have fucked up my life with drugs, but I was also extraordinarily self-aware. Anything I needed to talk about I had talked about. Unable to imagine wanting to return to that nightmarish part of my life, I'd been beyond Polly-anna-honest.

Seeing me chuckle he continued with, "Let's talk about 'Shaley the Great' for a bit." Yep, he brought that back from my time as a Serenity Lane in-patient. "Wow," I mumbled. My intent wasn't defiance but the absurdity of having to constantly question your reality was enough to make anyone feel unsure—borderline insane. "No, I think I'm OK. I realize I do possess a rather large ego at times, but I don't need to psychoanalyze 'Shaley the Great' anymore, Dave," I replied.

I understood where he and all the other counselors were coming from. I was a strange enigma in many ways. A lot of people finish 28 days of rehab and relapse within a few days or weeks. Most people need to attend regular meetings as the desire for drugs is very much alive and well, physically, or psychologically. I didn't seem to fit their typical model of addiction. And even though it was exhausting trying to convince them it was time for me to move on, I was finding great humor in the circular dance of it all. The more I insisted I was OK, the more it seemed I was in denial. "No, really, I'm OK. I swear!" would be met with a reverberating, "Denial." However, addiction was woven into the fabric of my being. So, I religiously attended meetings regularly, wanting to be certain I wasn't fooling myself. I knew firsthand that if given the chance, my addict mind would run amok down that slippery, denial-filled slope.

SEVENTEEN
WELCOME TO MY NEW LIFE

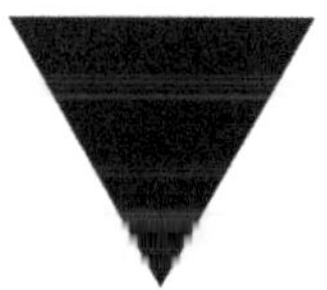

As they say in recovery, life continued "one day at a time." My business began to take off, finances improved, albeit sluggishly, and life seemed to be on an upward, positive, somewhat stable course. I had apologized and made amends to friends and family members so often they began to hide when they saw me coming. "We get it. We absolve you of your sins so please stop saying you're sorry," they'd joke.

Amy, whom I'd nicknamed Tiny because, well, she's tiny, constantly reminded whenever the opportunity presented itself, "I saved your life." She'd use this as a friendly form of faux guilt, especially when it came to getting treats. I'd get some sort of text asking, "Chocolate, please?" If I replied with a "no" text, my phone would immediately ping, "I saved your life." Her persistence annoyed the shit out of me. Some things never changed, I guess. God, I love her little manipulative butt.

Shortly after my release, Amy asked if I could help her with one of her properties. There was a storm passing through and the windows of her house needed to be covered with thick plastic due to water leakage. No problem, right? Unfortunately, in order to attach the plastic, we had to stand on extension ladders on either side of the windows about 10 feet up. I'm terrified of heights. Yep,

I have a fairly profound case of acrophobia so even the *thought* of getting on a ladder automatically makes my palms sweat. To make things even more trepidatious, the stormy wind and rain kept rushing in every few seconds, making balancing a challenge.

There's something about extension ladders that has always scared me. I think it's the combination of the horrendously loud clanking noise they make when they're ratcheted up and down, plus a feeling with one wrong move, I'd chop off a finger. But given that she'd "saved my life," I told her I'd push through it. I was also still fairly high on my "pink cloud" so my optimism tended to dominate. "This?!" I screamed over the howling wind. "This is a walk in the park on a sunny day! Come on, Tiny, we got this!"

We battened down one window successfully and had started in on the second when over the pelting rain, Amy shouted something to me about moving my ladder closer. This is the point in this story that I'd love to say I'm not the stereotypical lazy idiot but rather the person who *of course* did the safe, smart thing. Even if it meant getting down and repositioning my ladder. But alas, common sense was nowhere in sight that fine stormy day.

I proceeded to reach out, stretching my arm far across the wood shingles to the window frame, struggling to grab the plastic that angrily whipped back and forth in the wind. And wouldn't you know it, suddenly an enormous gust of wind swept underneath my ladder and pulled it back, away from the house. Amy froze—her face instantly pale, filled with panic, which told me everything I needed to know. I was going down.

The ladder proceeded to hover parallel to the house, like some clumsy Cirque du Solei act. I balanced there precariously in midair, slightly swaying but momentarily thinking I had dodged a bullet as the ladder seemed to be drifting back towards the house. Then the locking mechanism I was standing on gave way. Immediately I was jolted down three steps until abruptly I came to a jarring stop on the seventh rung. The impact of the lock catching was so sudden it forced my body backwards and I found myself gradually being pulled further away from the house. Before I could even scream, I was rapidly free falling. When the full force of gravity took hold, I was like an elephant falling from the clouds.

They say things happen in slow motion when you're about to meet your maker. That the story of your life passes like a movie, memory by memory in front of you. "Well, shit, this must be it," I thought, because time did seem to slow down. But only enough for me to think, "Seriously, Shaley. You are 'that guy' now. You could've just moved the ladder but instead, here you are, plummeting to your death." My peanut gallery's humor, with me till the end apparently.

I landed on my back with a muffled thud on top a stepping-stone. Not the soft mud that was everywhere else, but a hard, flat stone I'm certain I would've missed if I had actually aimed for it. Immediately there was a sharp, burning sensation in my chest. Gasping for breath I realized something was very wrong. I had knocked the wind out of me or possibly broken something. Amy rushed down and was trying to help as I writhed in pain on the muddy ground, unable to speak.

A woman across the street ran over, loudly informing us she had seen me fall and was a nurse. As I laid there, with a torrent of rain and mud splattering me, trying to take in her triage questions, all I kept thinking was, "She is so beautiful." Suddenly, I was acutely aware of my appearance and how disheveled I must've looked covered in mud like a wet ragdoll. My face transformed from twisted pain to glowing embarrassment. Amy, knowing me so well, said, "I think she'll be fine." Einstein's theory of relativity was spot on. Funny how intense my pain was prior to the arrival of the nurse neighbor. Then time did seem to slow, and my pain miraculously vanished the moment I gazed up at her face. Yeah, I'd survive.

Turned out, I'd broken a rib, which took weeks to heal but I managed to push through without pain medication. It was all relative. Compared to my childhood hardships, addiction, and especially the anguish growing up lesbian in a culture that hated lesbians—a broken bone paled in comparison. No matter what I'd been through, however, the world still hadn't changed much. At least around being gay. Lesbians, especially masculine looking ones, were still considered an ugly and deviant abnormality. And admittedly, there were moments when I contemplated if the homophobes were right. "I don't fit into this culture. Maybe I am a freakish aberration?"

One of the many positive by-products from rehab was learning how to closely examine and process my emotions. I became extremely self-aware. Up until then, I hadn't fully realized or acknowledged the depth of self-loathing and insecurities still weighing me down. Or how much I'd unwittingly continued to sabotage myself, listening to and validating lies that being gay was wrong. Being myself, was wrong. I dragged society's heteronormative trope around disguised as a close friend that would supposedly never lie to me. Convincing myself that the outside world, full of erroneous opinions was right, and my own voice was misguided.

It's funny, we know exactly who we are when we're young. But then the world around us starts to chip away, telling us how we're supposed to behave, what to wear, what's appropriate and not. Longing to fit in, we eagerly put up all sorts of façades, pretending to be what the world wants us to be. Years pass and soon our reflection in the mirror is a stranger. "Remember that little girl that didn't give a fuck what other people thought? The tomboy who loved being loud, and laughing hard without a care in the world? The girl that played in the dirt, caught tadpoles in the summer, and rode her bike until the streetlights came on? What happened to her?" We then begin a deliberate and liberating process of removing the masks and layers we applied over the years, searching for that girl who hadn't yet embraced conformity. That little girl lacking fear.

I'd spent an entire life pretending to be someone I wasn't, buying into the man-made idea of homophobia. Yet even with the self-awareness and healing I'd already achieved, undoing a lifetime of false personas takes time. At the age of 40, I continued to feel self-conscious and embarrassed in public as the out-of-place, awkward butch lesbian. People whispered, gave me sideways glances, and sometimes openly gawked without a hint of shame—as if knowing they belonged, and I didn't. Each time this happened, just as I'd been taught years before as a little girl, I'd try to appear more feminine in a futile attempt to draw less attention. Yes, at nearly six-feet tall, my response more-often-than-not *still*, was to hunch over and shrink to an acceptable five-foot-six, while muting my boisterous personality. Oh, and I'd start speaking three octaves higher, especially when entering public bathrooms.

When thinking back on that ridiculously fake, high-pitched voice, I always laugh, imagining kids running around at the mall, pulling their parent's arm, desperately searching for what was surely Barney the Dinosaur or Minnie Mouse making a cameo appearance. Upon seeing a big butch lesbian instead, their faces would fall with disappointment as they discovered I'm no "Minnie". Goofy maybe, but no Minnie. Yes, my self-indulging, cheesy sense of humor has always been an obvious camouflage attempting to hide any embarrassment and distress. Humor and laughter usually keep me buoyant. Unfortunately, the aftermath of trying to blend as a "normal" person, despite my silly levity, often ended in a volley of an internalized anger and a slew of self-deprecating thoughts.

The internal battle between my truth versus the lies I'd taken on as truth, continued. Although a pressing voice inside became harder to dismiss. Since coming out, I've tried to navigate two worlds; the LGBT world and the straight one, trying to fit into both. But the heteronormative world, by far the dominant one in this culture, was impossible to ignore. Yet ignoring who I was as a butch lesbian was also impossible. I found myself more often than not, denying my true self and surrendering to straight world standards. I felt as if I continually hovered in the space between, wanting to win people over. Straight people on one side, the LGBT community on the other. I wanted people to like and accept me in both worlds. But it was becoming painfully clear that my desire for people's acceptance of me, as the person I was, probably wasn't going to happen anytime soon.

A subtle "fuck you," kept peppering my thoughts, and slowly increased in volume, blatantly dismissing societies pressures for me to conform into their restrictive, heterosexual "box." A box I'd never been able to fit into in the first place. But I wasn't simply the lesbian "box" either. People aren't boxes to be checked off. Accompanying this newer defiant voice was a feeling of pride. Not just pride as in "I'm proud to be out and gay." It was a deeper acceptance and embracing of who I was as a complex human being. A human being who happened to be attracted to the same sex in a culture bound to binary ideology. The more defiant that inner voice became, the less weighted down I felt by my old feelings of shame. I began to feel comfortable in my own skin. When entering bathrooms, I decided to hold my head up high. "I belong here just as much as you do. Back the fuck off," I'd tell myself in a bold voice, edged with a slight rebellious, teenager undertone. But sophomoric tone or not, it worked and my confidence grew.

Internally, I felt like a dimmer light switch was slowly being pushed up, illuminating the darker areas of my mind. Eventually shining a light and revealing an inner wisdom that was there all along. I no longer needed any outside person—or for that matter, any internal protector, to validate my existence. I was part of the straight world *and* the LGBT world. I was even part of the space between. I was all of it. And I was fed up trying to live my life according to other people's standards.

EIGHTEEN

KAVORKA

I'd known for years that as a masculine-presenting lesbian, I was the antithesis of what feminine beauty was supposed to look like in our heteronormative culture. I'd tried to trivialize the hateful comments about my appearance and ignore the depth to which they affected me. *They're just small-minded, insecure assholes, Shaley. You should feel sorry for them.* I'd repeat those thoughts, opting for pity and superiority. In reality, the looks and comments often did hurt.

Now, however, with my new altered state of being, it seemed I rarely gave two shits what people thought about my sexual orientation or appearance. My new confidence was accompanied by a glowing sense of beauty and attractiveness. I'm not just talking about an inward attractive beauty. I'm talking outward, sex-appeal, "Ooh, baby, check me out," kind of beauty. OK, and inward beauty too.

I was flooded with a sense of self-love but also, self-*like*. Yes, I realized I actually *liked* myself. A lot. I was a strong, tall, handsome butch lesbian with a heart of gold that defied the mainstream concept of female beauty—a very *dull* concept of what beauty looked like, I might add. Also, I was funny. At least I thought so, which

I began to realize was ultimately much more important. Taking in this massive transformation, I grinned thinking, *Suck it, homophobes—I'm Shaley the Great and your hate mongering isn't working anymore!*

This new outer and inner beauty awareness was a double-edged sword, however. The upside was that I genuinely did feel all-around beautiful, like some sort of magnet people were drawn to. I'd always had a fairly infectious, fun-loving personality that people enjoyed, but this was bigger. My dating life began to sky-rocket. It was strange. Wherever I turned, there was some woman letting me know she thought I was attractive—especially younger women. That had never happened before. Never.

Admittedly, I did have moments of "fat headedness", as Amy called it, where my ego expanded to unfortunate heights. I literally developed a strut. An attempt at some sort of "sexy" swagger walk. In hindsight, what I thought was sexy probably appeared more like hip issues. Amy was certainly entertained. But come on, most of my life any compliments centered around my humor or how "cute" I was: never sexy or handsome. So, yeah, I reveled in it for a while. How refreshing and novel to be seen as beautiful. It didn't change who I was, but it still felt extraordinarily flattering.

For the life of me I have no clue why this shift happened. It just did. Maybe it was daily affirmations, never-ending AA meetings, or meditating in some uncomfortable yet enlightening lotus position. Perhaps it came from overcoming my experience with drugs, or a better understanding of my psychological childhood traumas. Perhaps it was some sort of spiritual aftermath of my awakening in rehab. But maybe, just *maybe*, my inner Shaley was fucking tired and fed up with a lifetime of feeling the need to apologize for being myself. Ultimately, it doesn't actually matter why it happened. It only mattered that it did. There's something very attractive about someone who feels 100% comfortable in their own skin.

I joked with Amy that I had a "Kavorka", a Latvian word for "the lure of the animal. In lay terms, suddenly it seemed like women were lusting after me. The downside to this newly discovered magnetism was the pendulum swung both ways, so perhaps a bit of a curse. When I was young and closeted, I'd watched this movie called, *American Gigolo* with Richard Gere. He played this hot young sex symbol who got paid to sleep with gorgeous women. All I did was fantasize and daydream about being his character, surrounded by hot women who not only desired me, but offered me money to be with them! One day, I realized that if I was some sought-after gigolo, yes, I might get paid to sleep with sexy women, but the more likely scenario would've involved me sleeping with whoever had cash for my services. Suddenly realizing this, my daydreams lost their titillating appeal. Even though attractive women were now seeking me out, there were many that weren't exactly welcome in my fantasies. Case in point.

Mary was a new client. It wasn't often my clients would be home when I was there, as the reason most hired me in the first place was to walk their dogs specifically when they were *not* home. For some unknown reason, though, Mary was able to work from home a great deal, and when she was there, she talked my ear off.

She was a single, middle-aged, high school counselor with two beautiful Shelties who were her world. Her charming bungalow had two tidy rows of marigolds and petunias seeming like a runway, guiding me to a bright, red front door framed with even more flowers. But it was the interior that could've easily rivaled Grandma's house. A potpourri of moth balls, Lysol, and mint permeated the air. Lace and dried flowers covered every surface. I mean *everything*. It was like there'd been some sort of monster sale at Joann Fabric and Mary cleaned them out. Lace doilies covered all the furniture. The end tables had doilies. The coffee table had doilies. Even the dining room table had doilies—over the lace tablecloth.

Sitting on top of the never-ending layers of lace were crystal bowls filled with hard candies that I'm sure had been collecting dust since the 1990s. Alongside each bowl stood a Victorian-era porcelain figurine whose sole purpose was to guard the candy. No matter where I moved, it felt like they were watching, just daring me to take a piece. "Go ahead. Try one. We promise you won't break a tooth." The only thing that seemed to be missing from Grandma's house was plastic to cover the furniture.

If Mary was home when I arrived, I'd almost always get cornered while she rattled on about everything—finances, administrative issues, unruly teenagers, and (of course) her beloved Shelties. For someone who had to keep a tight schedule of walking dogs, this was challenging. Eventually it got to the point that if I pulled up and saw her car in the driveway, I'd yell an elongated, "Fuck me!" and add an extra 20 minutes to that stop. Enough time to listen to Mary's woes.

This continued more frequently over time, Mary suffocating me with her uninvited monologues and incessant complaining. I tried to stay positive and not be resentful towards her, but I was a captive audience. It did cross my mind that I should seriously consider charging extra for armchair therapy. Being a somewhat compassionate person, I reminded myself that she was just a lonely human being that had no one else to talk to. That worked for a while.

One day I walked into her always-tidy house to find a pair of fuzzy blue handcuffs, that's right, *handcuffs*, sitting conspicuously on her lacey white dining room tablecloth. *Nope.* I thought. *Just here to walk dogs.* I decided that they were not intended for my eyes, there was some logical reason they were in plain sight, and what Mary did in her personal life was none of my business. That's what I kept repeating to myself as I quickly headed out with her dogs in tow.

My peanut gallery was instantly catapulted into a raucous cacophony of opinions. Outside me was desperately trying to calmly give Mary the benefit of a doubt and stay out of it. But the imaginary, smart-ass, obvious voice of reason, Mr. Samuel L. Jackson, kept yelling, "Are you fucking kidding me? You've got to be fucking kidding me! Those handcuffs were meant for your eyes and I'm telling you, you do *not* want to stick around to see why! Walk those dogs and get your butch ass out of here!" My exit from her house that day was, let's just say—quick.

On my next visit, there was no Mary in sight, so I thought the coast was clear. My relief was short-lived however as she popped out from her hallway, cornered me, and proceeded to tell me about her dating life. I was sweating as I struggled to quickly grab and leash up her squirming, overly excited dogs, desperately trying to escape. Undeterred by my obvious discomfort, she followed me, elaborating even more about the date she was going on that night. "That's great, Mary!" I spat as I dashed out the door with her dogs.

Upon my return, she continued rambling on as if I never left. She asked if she could show me something and then ran out of the living room, not waiting for my reply. I stood there silently, letting out a sigh of frustration, nostrils flaring. A wave of absolute dread consumed me. Wanting to be polite, although by then I'm not sure why, I stood there patiently. She was a human being and, more importantly, a client. A client among only a handful at the time. My hand rested on the front doorknob, ready to flee, as I waited with trepidation for what Mary was going to whip out for show-n-tell. At this point, Samuel L. Jackson was having a field day, "What the hell is wrong with you? The time is now; nobody wants to see what Grandma has to show you!"

I foolishly ignored him and waited. Mary returned with a shoebox and pulled out stiletto heels and fishnet stockings. She stood there flashing her black, fishnet stockings and spikey fuck-me pumps then unabashedly asked my opinion. Of course, my first thought was, "I am your dog walker, and a rather *butch* dog walker whose closet consists of flannel. *Lots of flannel.* And furthermore…" Samuel interrupted my thoughts and yelled, "Furthermore, Mary, why yes, that sleazy would-be Halloween costume you're thinking of wearing is both becoming and absolutely age appropriate! I'm sure your dog walker wants to hear all about it!" All I said was, "You'll look great!"

Knowing full well Samuel L. Jackson was simply part of my elaborate choir of voices, I had to admit he, or me, or all of us were having this strange, overlapping, multi-opinionated inner dialogue. He may have been crude in his delivery, but the message was spot on. It was what I'd been dying to openly say for the longest time. His version was just in a more, well…in-your-face, "fuck you" style. I imagined my more appropriate and less volatile response would've been, "I am your dog walker. Not your therapist. Not your fashion consultant. Your damn dog walker so please leave me alone." None of that was said though as I forced a smile and attempted to exit.

But Mary wasn't finished. She stopped me again and giddily announced how excited she was about her party adding, "I might even play with a woman!" All that was missing was a creepy wink. My jaw dropped and skin crawled. I turned slowly, opened the door, and left without saying a word—head spinning with confusion. *Holy shit, is she attracted to me? Was that flirting?* Yes, admittedly I was a bit slow from a lifetime of not being the belle of the ball. All I kept thinking as I ran to my car was, *Shut it, Sam. Not a word.*

Weeks went by before I saw or heard anything from Mary, which was an enormous relief. I thought maybe she'd developed the good sense to be embarrassed and was off somewhere cringing at her unsolicited behavior. Since nothing unusual had happened since the "I might play with a woman" day, I figured it was a one-time, bizarre thing, even by Mary standards.

A few weeks later, I received a text from her asking if I could walk her dogs that evening. I asked her what time, and she told me 6:00p.m. would be great. I agreed and thought nothing of it. She started to tell me her plans to go to Multnomah Falls with some man she met. Before she could share more, I cut her off with, "I'll make sure the dogs are taken care of," and hit send.

At 6:00p.m., I pulled up to her house and saw her car in the driveway. It was strange, but I figured maybe she drove with someone else. I walked up to the door and let myself in without thinking to knock because, why would I? I am a dog walker, so people give me their keys to go in their house because again, they're usually not home when they ask me to walk their dogs.

I opened the door and was slammed back by her two Shelties, who seemed to be pleading, "Please help us! Get us out of here!" They were both panting heavily, frantically jumping around the entrance that was littered with empty beer cans. Grandma's house with empty beer cans scattered *anywhere?* That should've been my first clue to run away.

I looked up to see Mary, half-naked in front of her fireplace, doing a strip tease for some crusty old man who had a Cheshire Cat grin plastered on his face. Mary turned to me and with feigned surprise exclaimed, "Oh, Shaley! What are you doing here?" I stood there dumbfounded and frozen, desperate to erase the image of her half-naked body forever burned into my retinas. Meanwhile the man sitting on her couch kept smiling and staring—possibly drooling. Somehow, I managed to stutter, "Um, you asked me to walk your dogs' tonight?"

Unsure what to do, I just stood there for what seemed like an eternity. Then as if on some weird polite autopilot sequence, I found myself walking over to the man, hand extended for an introduction. I mean, I *certainly* wouldn't have wanted anyone to feel uncomfortable or awkward without proper introductions. This was so me to pretend, "Why yes, this sort of thing happens all the time. It's no big deal. Don't mind me while you're stripping. I'm just gonna take the dogs out for a walk. Oh, and I didn't catch your name, creepy couch man. I'm Shaley."

My peanut gallery was ballistic: laughing, yelling, and I think there was a bit of blood curdling screaming in the background. I'd also developed tunnel vision as I tried to focus and stumbled back towards the doorway. After I had made my proper salutations of course.

At that point I turned to leave immediately, but Mr. Jackson yelled, "Leave the invoice! Unless you want to come back for another show, leave the damn invoice!" In a daze, I turned around one last time to see Mary standing there in a clumsy half-hearted attempt to cover her bulging breasts, the stalker-like man grinning, and the poor dogs clamoring at the door for an escape. Doing my best to be invisible, I turned slowly and whispered loudly, "I'm just gonna leave this here," letting the invoice fall on top of the empty beer cans.

Racing back to my car, I rechecked my messages thinking perhaps I had screwed up the timing or the day Mary had wanted me to come over. But there was no mistake on my part; Mary had planned the whole disturbing event. The next morning, she sent me a text which read, "I hope you weren't embarrassed last night. *We* weren't!"

Yes, finally knowing what it was like to be attractive and desirable was thrilling at times. But other times, not so much. And even though I needed the business, it was painfully obvious Mary needed to go. On some level, despite the whole awkward and unwelcome ordeal, I was grateful. Maybe I couldn't pick and choose who was attracted to me, but at least I was *finally* considered attractive. For a kid growing up in this culture as a would-be gay ugly duckling, I felt like I had arrived.

My first true love Amy and me out camping.

Amy and me at San Francisco Pride, screwing around as now BFF's.

Beverly, Amy and me at their wedding ceremony when same-sex marriage passed in 2015!

Geri and Dad supporting my Human Rights Campaign Event.

Amy, me, Dad, Geri and Grandma Betty at Portland Pride marching with PGLAG. Amy and I were BFF's by then and everyone was having fun, trying to get me a date.

Laurie, Cynthia, Darcelle, Mom, and me attending the legendary Darcelle XV.

Me, Beth and Laurie
at a Go-Go's summer
Concert.

Beth, Cynthia, Me
and Laurie in a
family photo. (Lots
of hair)

Timbers FC Billboard! Such an honor! And how I ended up meeting Snapper!

The first time I met Snapper. Hands down, the sweetest and smartest little kid. And DAPPER!

Snapper as a teenager. Still sweet and smart but so grown up now!

NINETEEN

OH, FOR FUCK'S SAKE, I'M A WOMAN

Walking a client's dog one afternoon, I noticed a stray dog a few blocks ahead with no owner in sight. I'd seen off-leash dogs wreak havoc upon leashed-up ones in the past, so I was immediately in high alert mode. Adding to my concern, I was walking Pepper, a dog I knew had serious dog aggression in general and wouldn't be happy with a wandering stray dog provoking her. I started scanning the streets for the owner in a frantic attempt to avoid a massive canine confrontation.

I spotted a young teenager in a baggy sweatshirt and beanie glued to his phone on the other side of the street. "Hey, kid! Do you know who that dog belongs to?" I shouted. He glanced up at me and then yelled dismissively, "Not my dog, Grandpa!" without the slightest interruption in stride. Maybe it was simply because he was a teenager that I received such an abrupt, uninterested response. Or perhaps it was because I called him a kid? At my age, though, with crow's feet carving the corners of my eyes, everyone under 25 seems like a kid to me.

But it was hearing "Grandpa" that did me in. Over the years of being misgendered I'd been called mister, dude, sir, brah and even "dad" to my dog. But "Grandpa" made me stop in my tracks and laugh. Maybe it was my gray hair and masculine appearance? It was definitely a first.

As a seriously muscular woman, OK, a *sort of* muscular woman, with a large stature, fauxhawk, and chiseled jaw, I have the pleasure of being misgendered often. It wasn't new to me. Whether in a public setting, entering bathrooms, or even from my own clients, it happened *a lot*. I'd learned to roll with it most of the time because what's the alternative? To scream and yell every time it happened? I would've been exhausted. But when people misgendered me intentionally or showed no obvious regret, it sometimes felt unbearable.

Not long after the "Grandpa" incident, I was leaving the mall walking back to my car. Mind you, I was just in a mall, and if you're like me—malls in general are hell on earth. They're crowded and prey upon our insecurities, convincing us that having certain material things will bring happiness to our dreary lives. They are also the epitome of heteronormative culture. And if you're a masculine presenting, tall lesbian in suburbia mall USA, consider yourself a deer on the first day of hunting season. So, having just exited this mall and trying to shake off the never-ending stares, I wasn't in the best of moods.

As I approached my car, two women across the parking lot started yelling, "Oh my *God*, is that a man or woman?" They were laughing hysterically because, apparently, it's hilarious to launch insults at complete strangers. Something in me snapped. I mean, why not? I was already feeling shitty, so apparently it was on. Flushing with outrage I shouted, "Come say that to my face!" while aggressively waving them over.

My peanut gallery, suddenly awake, stared on in pure astonishment at my response, wondering what on earth I was doing. Looking back, I'm not exactly sure what I was trying to accomplish. It just felt so damn good to say something instead of taking it like I'd done so often.

Both of their faces froze with surprise. I don't think they were expecting a response and certainly not one with an invitation to, what—duke it out? I, myself, was a bit confused. I clearly wasn't thinking things through, but I also didn't care. I was tired, and *definitely* tired of feeling bullied. Isn't it enough to have to go inside a mall, feeling like some circus window display, without the added bonus of harassment outside too? A person can only take so much.

Luckily for me, there was no ridiculous ensuing brawl. Hearing my response, they immediately jumped into their car and sped away. I can only imagine the story they told their friends afterwards, "Oh my *God*, you won't believe what just happened! This ginormous 7-foot-tall man-woman attacked us out of nowhere!" I walked away regretful for losing my temper, but happy my outburst did make them run for the suburban hills and no one got hurt. Well, no one got physically hurt.

The following winter, close to the holidays, I was having one of those days. We all have them; days where the only thing we long for is to crawl back under our warm covers. My patience was zero to none as I was overly fatigued and ready to call it quits. I'd been out all-day walking dogs in a steady cold downpour, the kind that soaks you to the bones and teaches you the difference between "water-resistant" and "waterproof" gear. My feet were throbbing and all I kept dreaming about was a warm shower. But the universe had one more fun event planned on that cold December day: the post office.

There I stood, in a packed, muggy room, lined with people holding their precious (albeit soaked) parcels. I could feel my wet jeans and raincoat sticking to my skin as we shuffled sluggishly like the walking dead—dripping and miserable. My head was buried in my phone as I longed for distraction and escape, eager to hear the word, "Next!"

And I did hear it. But what I heard before it was, "Sir! You're next, *sir*." I looked up, wishing for there to be someone in front of me that would be the obvious "sir" but found no one. I was the sir. Already in an irritable, short-tempered mood, I found myself foolishly scanning my surroundings, hoping to tell an actual "sir" that the next window was open.

With no other person standing there, the postal agent's voice seemed to increase in volume and agitation, "Sir, are you ready?" At this point, the people waiting in line were visibly uncomfortable as almost everyone suddenly realized what was happening. Any mumbling conversations stopped abruptly, and eyes became glued to phone screens in a desperate attempt to avoid the instant palpable tension filling the air.

"Sir?" I heard again in an almost semi-scolding tone—like an exasperated, weary teacher with no more patience. I looked up hoping for the love of God, when I finally made eye contact, the agent would see their mistake and apologize. Nope. They continued with "Sir?" looking directly at me. There was nowhere to hide. Every single person in that post office was cringing. I'd had a long, tiresome day, and the last thing I wanted was to be thrown unwillingly into the spotlight. *Oh, for fuck's sake. I am a woman, dammit. Don't you see? But fine, let's dance.*

I stepped towards the counter while everyone in line slowly took two steps back. Taking a deep breath, I looked directly at the agent and said politely, "Are you referring to me? Because if you are, I'm not a "sir." I'm a woman. And honestly, I don't like being called sir or ma'am. So, here's an idea—let's just lose the pronouns if you're unsure. Maybe just say 'next customer please'?" As if I could see the lightbulb flicker on, the agent blushed and nodded, then hurriedly slid my package across the counter.

I've always had a sizable selection of opinionated people in the peripheral of my life. People who "know better" than me when it comes to how to say things, when to say things, if it's my place to say things, and so on. When it comes to correcting people, I've heard it all, "But, Shaley, putting someone on the defensive for misgendering you is the wrong way to make progress." To those people I say, "No way. I'm only human and can only take so much before hitting that age-old 'straw that broke the camel's back'."

Whether it's micro-aggressions or outright bullying, why does the responsibility to educate or coddle others rest on the shoulders of the oppressed? It is not my job to tiptoe around them, even if their unsolicited discrimination and oppression flows out of ignorance. To be fair, I did practice a modicum of restraint. I could've gone off the deep end but chose instead to simply give the agent a strongly worded alternative. Believe me, I chose to ignore a whole arsenal of obscenities my peanut gallery was lobbying at me.

My experiences with being misgendered haven't always ended with anger and resentment. There have definitely been situations where I've seen people at their best. Like the time I was waiting at the grocery deli to pick out my lunch. The attendant asked the usual, "Yes, what can I get you?" But of course added, "Sir." Before I could even respond, an older woman in a matching plastic floral print rain bonnet and jacket corrected the clerk, "This is not a 'sir.' This is a woman." I hadn't even noticed her standing there prior to hearing her speak.

I managed to close my half-opened mouth, which was programmed to automatically respond when feeling attacked. She glanced up at me, while I stood blushing slightly, feeling dumbfounded and unsure. This was new. Then she smiled and motioned for me to order. Her small act of kindness, after being misgendered so often in life and always feeling like an outsider, meant the world to me. I felt a lump in my throat as I tried to swallow. Then with teary eyes I turned to order.

Maybe that tiny-framed woman had experienced a lifetime of her own personal oppression and knew firsthand the importance of standing up for others. Who knows? Maybe she sensed an impending altercation and wanted to quash it before it became something that would delay her ability to order. Whatever her motive, I left with misty eyes and a renewed sense of hope, along with a container full of macaroni.

Sometimes, even when being misgendered stings, I've learned to choose my battles. One early morning I was waiting inside a Chevron station, attempting to pay. The gas attendant walked in, demanding a receipt for another patron. The woman behind the counter curtly responded with, "I'm with a customer." Then without any warning, they started yelling at each other as if I wasn't there. He first demanded, "I need it now!" adding, "You don't even know what you're doing!" Followed with her screaming that, "You're the one who has no clue what you're doing, so shut up!" My head began to bob back and forth like I was watching a reality TV tennis match.

I instinctively took a step back from the counter as this "conversation" became more like a John McEnroe meltdown. Glancing around to see if anyone else was witnessing the ordeal, I realized I was the only customer in the store. I had a $20 bill in hand and was intrigued, but rapidly sensing the need to flee. They were almost circling each other like snarling rabid dogs. *Should I be cheering? Should I brace myself for racket throwing or, in this case, air-born cherry slushies?*

Out of nowhere, the cashier looked up and paused in the middle of her shouting, as if seeing me for the first time to say, "I'm so sorry, *Sir*". Then the gas attendant, also mid-yell, interrupted his own tirade to reiterate the apology, "Yes, excuse us, Sir." Not sure exactly what I should do, I stuttered a questioning, "Um, yeah, no problem?" and laid my money on the counter. Hearing the door chime as I slowly backed out, not daring to take my eyes off them until reaching my car, I reminded myself: there are obvious times to correct people and then there are times to just leave it alone.

By far, the most entertaining misgendering incident was with my clients Bob and Betty. They were a sweet, older retired coupled that reminded me of matching salt and pepper shakers. They sported identical sweat suits, gray hair, and glasses. It was Bob that typically greeted me, as Betty was usually out and about, preoccupied with a variety of hobbies. Bob was lucid most of the time but sometimes…not so much. But he was always pleasant, and usually gave me a vague morning, "Welcome," while I leashed up their dogs.

Because he was hard of hearing, I would always announce myself loudly when entering the house, not wanting to accidentally surprise him. Sometimes he'd be fully dressed, and other times he'd be wearing some sort of adult diaper and undershirt, as if pants slipped his mind. I'm not sure if he actually forgot them or was simply more comfortable in his underwear, or perhaps at a certain age you just stop caring. Each time it happened I decided to just go with it, because, why not? He was never perverse, just a bit senile. Anyway, I was there to walk the dogs, not him.

One summer day, I arrived to see Bob in the kitchen (complete with pants, fortunately) making toast and eggs. When I entered, he looked up and with an enormous smile yelled, "Good day to you, Sir! So glad you're here to walk these rascals. They're excited for their morning walk." I stood there unsure what to say. I'd been walking their dogs every weekday for over two years. Staring up at him, I wondered if he'd always thought I was a man or if on that particular day he had forgotten who I was. Either way, all I could think of to respond with was, "Well good morning to you, good Sir! I am more than happy to take care of them!"

Maybe as we age gender becomes irrelevant? Or maybe he had dementia? Maybe he just never figured out years before if I was male or female, and had personally decided on male? Laughing as I walked out with their miniature poodles I thought, "I really need to write this stuff down."

My biggest challenge as far back as I can remember has always been public bathrooms. People have followed me inside informing me I'd entered the wrong bathroom because of course, they know. They wouldn't bother asking politely if I was male or female, they simply assumed. Even asking, however, would be a presumption that I'm interested in sharing my gender identity, or an insinuation I might be confused. To be so righteously arrogant, entitled, and borderline confrontational with a stranger never ceased to astound me.

Coming back from one particularly exhausting flight, I went into the bathroom at the Dallas airport. As I entered the bathroom, a woman followed me in exclaiming, "Sir...*sir*...this is the women's bathroom." A bit dazed and overly fatigued my body sank. I turned hoping she'd immediately see her error, blush with embarrassment, and slink away. Undeterred, she continued her mission to enforce and protect the sanctity of binary bathroom norms. "This is the women's bathroom, not the men's," she continued. I stared directly in her eyes and for probably the 12,000th time in my life said, "I *am* a woman." Due to my sleep deprivation, however, my sensitivity chip was MIA, so I grabbed my boobs and added, "And I'm more of a woman than you'll ever be!" She stood motionless and, thankfully, silent, as I turned and entered the stall.

After my inner applause subsided at my witty response, I realized that *prior* to that interaction, I was so dead tired that I had originally, fully walked into the men's bathroom before realizing I was in the wrong one—and then walked over to the women's. So, if she had seen that, it might have confused her. But by then, I didn't care. I was tired. And *definitely* tired of being misgendered. Sitting on the toilet I sighed quietly, "For fuck's sake, who made you the bathroom police lady?" Then my sigh turned into a laugh as my peanut gallery added, "But seriously, did you see her face when you grabbed your boobs? Priceless. Well done, babe."

TWENTY

I'M STILL STANDING

A few months after rehab, I happily offered to go to the dump with Amy one day. "Who are you and what have you done with my friend Shaley?" she joked with a smirk adding, "Actually, I like this Shaley better—the other one was a pain in my ass." Yes, people who'd known me for years suddenly thought I was some sort of alien imposter. My outward appearance and core personality remained the same, but it was obvious my perspective on life had shifted dramatically.

The combination of everything; growing up gay in a hostile, homophobic world, childhood trauma, and drug addiction, had climaxed into a perfect tornado-like storm. I felt like the cow in the movie *Twister*. "I gotta go, Julia, we got cows." Yep, I was that out-of-control cow being chaotically tossed around at frightening speeds until I lost "udder" control. Cue rehab. The flip side of that nightmarish storm was it transformed my life. It spat me out at my ultimate rock bottom forcing some sort of monumental watershed moment. I felt alert and clear with purpose, as if some sort of call-ing or internal compass was guiding me, focused on community instead of my own self-absorbed existence. I was eager to help change the world somehow, even in a small way.

But wanting to change the world and changing it are two entirely different beasts. The world seemed overflowing with insurmountable problems. If I hadn't felt inept and small before my awakening, I certainly felt so after taking off my rose-colored glasses. I was suddenly aware why so many people choose to look the other way and feign ignorance. It felt hopeless. Seriously, how the hell do people change the world? From an individualist point of view, it seemed heartbreakingly daunting.

But isn't that part of the problem? It's the age-old conundrum we struggle with: how can any *one* person change the world? I certainly didn't have the answer. What I did know, or rather one thing that was fucking drilled into me from rehab, was just take one baby step at a time. *"Rome wasn't built in a day. One person may not be able to change the world alone, but hey, you could certainly start…maybe others would join?"* I thought laying on my bed, staring out at the morning rain. *"But move, Shaley—take a step. Better yet, take a shower, then take a step."*

I decided my first step would be to volunteer. When in doubt, help others. I joined organizations that focused on LGBTQ and women's issues because—well, duh. My perspective of the world and priorities may have shifted, but the social issues that remained close to my heart were the same. My desire was to show others, especially other queers, that they weren't alone. I had silently suffered for years, feeling alienated, depressed, and lost in a culture that intentionally and systematically led me to believe I was abnormal. I couldn't recall one positive queer role model growing up that I could have turned to for guidance and reassurance.

Even if I had wanted to drop all my burgeoning "let's save the world" desires, it was impossible. They were now fully part of who I was. I had this exciting, sometimes strangely nervous energy that vibrated throughout my body. I may have been a little bit late, but I'd finally arrived at my own party—thrilled to be there but unsure what the night would hold. I knew that as a proud, out-spoken, very visible butch lesbian, living a normal life despite the heteronormative world around me, would have a positive impact. At a bare minimum, simply by showing up I'd at least be a living example to other LGBTQ people that, yes, we are normal.

The years that followed didn't disappoint. Through all my hard work, volunteering, and community endeavors, I received a plethora of recognition for my efforts. Admittedly, this is where my ego, again, did start to inflate. Even after losing everything and hitting a humiliating rock bottom, my ego still somehow survived. Fortunately, when I'd start pouting because I hadn't received my "due credit" or accolades for some event I'd created, Amy was there with her tiny violin, always quick to put things in perspective.

"Well, why are you doing these community events?" she'd ask, "Are you doing them because you want fat-headed attention and notoriety, or because you actually care and want to help others?" God, my ego hated her. The answer, of course, was because I cared. If something I did, big or small, helped others in my community, then mission accomplished.

I was extremely grateful and fortunate to receive awards over time for my volunteer efforts. Let's face it, volunteering is often a thankless job. Even being *noticed* as a volunteer is an accomplishment in and of itself. Volunteers do the crap jobs like tearing down events and picking up after others. Being part of these events taught me to appreciate the countless people who routinely showed up and did the shit no one else wanted to do.

I did, I admit, enjoy some of the attention. Not necessarily because I was fat-headed as Amy suggested (although a tiny piece of me did revel in the spotlight). Mainly, it was because the other side of that notable attention brought more visibility. The accolades and recognition I received were accompanied with a noticeable platform. And shit, I *wanted* other LGBTQ people, struggling and doubting their worth, to see an openly gay butch lesbian living an ordinary life. Walking through the world with pride. I wanted to be an example of someone who, through a lifetime of personal tragedy and struggles, had realized that being queer was actually quite normal. Possibly boring.

In 2015 I was chosen to be on the Timbers FC billboard. To anyone outside of Oregon, we are football (aka soccer) fanatics and *love* our Timbers FC. So being chosen to be on a Timbers FC billboard was a big deal. And talk about a boost in butch visibility. There I was, after a lifetime of thinking I was ugly and weird, being praised from an outside admirer as, "all that and then some." The billboard was me posing with two axes, muscles bulging and a stone-serious face. Almost as if I was saying, "That's right, bitches, I'm a badass butch lesbian. Deal with it." Whoever took the photo, however, should get more credit. The billboard image definitely made me look much more ripped and intimidating than I am. It's apparently all in the lighting, but I'll take it.

Amy went with me to check out the billboard when it first went up, and I literally stood there frozen, grinning ear to ear, stunned. I was flooded with memories of the countless nights I'd spent crying myself to sleep, begging the universe for an answer as to why I was born this way. And there was my 25-foot glorious answer, "Because you are a beautiful butch lesbian and now the world will know."

OK, maybe it wasn't that *Lion King*, "Circle of Life" dramatic. But it was definitely a full-circle moment that made me proud. I felt like I had not only survived, but I had persevered and won. My community achievements and accolades—combined with a towering billboard—thrust me onto an even larger, and literally more visible, platform. It was a good day to be gay.

Not long after the billboard went up, I received an unusual email from a client asking me if I'd meet with her friend's 10-year-old daughter who was struggling. Her name was Snapper and she had recently come out as lesbian. Immediately I replied with, "Of course!" As it turned out, Snapper wasn't just gay, she was a little baby butch. And she was absolutely adorable.

I pulled up to their home in the Northwest Hills and through my dirt-speckled windshield glimpsed this kid on a balcony overlooking the street. Dressed in a navy blue, crisp short-sleeve shirt (buttoned all the way up to her chin) and matching Bermuda shorts, she smiled down sheepishly as I pulled into the driveway. Then she vanished. Even with my windows up I could hear, "She's here, Mom! She's here!" Laughing to myself, and not quite sure what I was walking into, I parked and headed to the front door.

A tall woman with long light brown hair and kind eyes answered the door, introducing herself as Jaimee, Mom, while Snapper peered around her, blushing. Have you ever just wanted to squeeze a little kitten or puppy because they are so insanely cute? That's how I felt with Snapper. I just wanted to squeeze her! She was the sweetest little kid on the planet, with rosy plump cheeks, a short combed over haircut, and dimples that landed her decidedly in the "Cute Overload" category.

"Welcome!" Jaimee said as she motioned me inside. Turning to Snapper, I put out my hand and said, "It is a pleasure to meet you. I love your outfit! Very dapper!" This brought on a huge smile she was clearly trying to contain, followed by a quiet, "Thank you." Jaimee lovingly laughed and said, "She changed her outfit five times before you arrived and at one point had on a tux." It took everything I had to conceal my reaction. My heart was nearly bursting with adoration and love. This little girl was so excited to meet me, knowing *nothing* about me other than the fact that I was on a billboard. But it should've been obvious, at least to me: I looked like her.

We sat down and Jaimee started the conversation casually, asking Snapper if she had any questions for me. Snapper went into kid-shy mode, avoiding eye contact and plucking invisible fibers from the fancy throw pillows. Then Jaimee did what moms are great at: she asked polite, yet probing questions of us both. Still reeling from the initial greeting, I began offering up basic information about myself. All the boring background stuff like where I'm from, what I do, how long I've been out, if I have a girlfriend etc., hoping the ice would crack. Then Jaimee asked Snapper pointedly, "So, you definitely consider yourself a lesbian?" "Yep. I'm gonna marry a woman someday," came Snapper's prompt response. "You don't see yourself as possibly transgender or bisexual?" Jaimee asked casually. "No, Mom. I told you. I'm a lesbian."

I sat there in silent astonishment. This 10-year old kid must have been the bravest person I knew. Although soft spoken, the depth of her self-awareness and maturity, knowing clearly who she was at such a young age, was remarkable. I was dumbfounded. *Fucking incredible.* She was like a *far* more advanced little mini-me. I was blown away and trying to process everything, but still not quite understanding why I was there. Finally, the light bulb went off. *Duh, Shaley, she may be a courageous young kid, but homophobia and transphobia still loom everywhere.*

In our relaxed back and forth conversation on a variety of everyday topics, it finally came to light that Snapper was sometimes bullied and misgendered in school. In her world, she looked and possibly acted different than most girls her age. And being an out lesbian, I'm sure she was an easy target. This sort of ridicule left her feeling isolated and alone. It's too much for a ten-year-old kid. Really, it's often too much for grown adults. This I understood.

"You know," I started, "Being a butch lesbian and having a very masculine appearance, I've been teased a lot in life. And I still get misgendered all the time." As I said this, I caught a sliver of a smile appear then quickly disappear. "Well, what do you do when they call you a boy?" she asked. "It depends, I guess. Usually, people are just ignorant and oblivious, so I correct them and tell them I'm female. Most people are slightly embarrassed and apologize quickly," I said. Then added, "But you know, some people are just jerks. Ignore them if you can. They're just insecure and need to make others feel bad."

The conversation continued and she invited me to see her room. I'd forgotten what a big deal it was to show other people the cool shit in your room, especially adults. Unfortunately, I literally have no memory of what she showed me. It seemed almost surreal that I was in this stranger's house, listening to a young butch excitedly rattle on about whatever cool stuff kids were into. I had a few moments of holding back tears as the entire situation overwhelmed me. I had known I wanted to be a role model and help other LGBTQ people, but I always thought it would be more in line with visibility and the creation of community events. It never crossed my mind that I'd be an in-person, giant mirror for a young butch lesbian.

As I started to head out, it was hard not to notice the ease with which Snapper and Jaimee playfully bantered back and forth. Snapper, who kept giggling at Jaimee's teasing, seemed so relaxed, as if she knew no matter what, she was fully accepted with her family. And Jaimee, who was clearly overflowing with love and support of her child, was making sure Snapper knew, no matter what, she was safe with her. Their interactions immediately brought back images of my mom. We had such a complicated relationship, but she had loved me unconditionally when it came to who I was as a person. That much I knew. She loved me wherever I stood under the LGBTQ rainbow. In fact, I knew at my core, she could've cared less if I was straight, lesbian, non-binary, transgender…none of that mattered to her. She had always simply seen me as her beautiful child in that sense. And in that way, she was my biggest fan.

After we said our goodbyes and took the obligatory selfies, I drove away suddenly flushed with childhood memories. After all those years being closeted, feeling isolated and never fitting in, it truly did feel like a "Circle of Life" moment so, whatever, cue *Lion*

King. It certainly hadn't been an easy road growing up butch, more like death by a thousand paper cuts. A lifetime filled with snide laughs, grimaces, and sneers. No matter how much I'd tried to fit in, I was still always the "other." The outcast.

Yet through a myriad of painful experiences, at some point I had learned I could choose my own path. I could choose how I wanted to react. I could boil over with anger and resentment or remove my armor and let love take over. Because love was my source. It had *always* been my source. I *was* little Snapper. I was that same scared young girl longing to be seen and loved for who she was. And who knows? Perhaps all those struggles I faced and every lesson learned had inadvertently helped. Maybe, just maybe, I had shared some tiny nugget of wisdom with Snapper that could help her navigate through the challenging times she would face simply for being different.

As I watched Snapper and her mom wave goodbye in my rearview mirror, a memory popped into my mind from the mid-1990s. Amy and I had decided to get tattoos while visiting San Francisco. For this virgin tattoo experience, we chose the lesbian owned Black and Blue Tattoo. Amy had been contemplating her design for years and had detailed instructions and drawings outlining exactly what she wanted. She was always the planner. I, of course, had no plan. All I knew for sure was all the cool kids had tattoos, and if Amy was getting one, I wanted one too. And it had to be an arm band. It was the '90s. Arm bands were a thing, especially with lesbians.

To some people, having something permanently tattooed might be a weighty choice and lengthy process. Not for this impulsive butch. I immediately thought of a quote that had always resonated with me, part of which was, "Be true to yourself and be free." It was a gut reaction, but the decision felt right. The full version of the quote I had in mind was rather lengthy so, regrettably, fitting the entire quote around my bicep wasn't going to work. At least not in a font large enough to see with the naked eye. Apparently, my perception of my bicep girth and the reality of my actual bicep size were vastly different.

The tattoo artist I chose was this radical looking lesbian, adorned with colorful tattoos and short, spikey hair. I showed her my lengthy quote and explained how I wanted it tattooed in one line around my bicep. She sat across the glass counter case, filled with an array of art, completely silent. Then she looked over at my arm while I discreetly flexed my muscles. Her eyes moved from my pseudo-inflated bicep back to my face.

This wordless communication continued until I got the feeling she was thinking, "Honey, puff up your bicep all you want but I'm still not a miracle worker." Not wanting to accept reality, but realizing arguing with her was futile, I reluctantly took the silent hint. "You know what? I changed my mind," I announced, as if it had been my idea all along, "short and sweet is better. Right to the point. 'Be True to Yourself and Be Free' is perfect." Then, nervously, I whispered, "You can fit those seven words, right?"

It had been almost 25 years since I'd gotten that tattoo. Driving home, I glanced down at the now faded, blurred cursive wrapped around my slowly sagging arm. It struck me how those simple seven words had been so insightful and appropriate. It was almost as if the all-knowing inner me had been trying to spell out the answer years ago, in an attempt to ease my suffering by tattooing it on my body. How many times had I stumbled around, painfully lost in life? My little Buddha Buddy Amy would always remind me, "Oh, for fuck's sake, read your arm if you want to know the answer." Did I listen? Of course not.

I'd been desperately pleading for answers from the universe for years, only to feel more and more isolated and ignored in the silence that followed. Yet the universe *had* been listening, I simply hadn't been able to hear it. My poor guardian angel must have been exhausted. "I'm done. I'm out. I have literally—lit-er-all-y—

tattooed the answer on her body and she still missed it. I'm out. I'll get my wings next year."

There is a vast difference between a cerebral understanding that you are complete, loved, and perfect, versus an internal, perhaps spiritual, knowing. Sitting at the intersection, I wondered… if my often-tumultuous life, laden with pain, *hadn't* been riddled with suffering, would any level of this profound self-actualization have manifested?

A honking car behind me broke the "Deep thoughts with Shaley Howard", moment and I laughed *Fuck, who cares?* I mean, really, I'll most likely never know the answers to these esoteric questions and, ultimately, it simply didn't matter why. It only mattered that it did happen. It became obvious in that moment that being authentic to who I was, despite whatever the world threw at me, was and had always been my path to freedom. It didn't matter what outsiders thought of me, it only mattered what I thought of myself. "Be True to Yourself and Be Free." Short and sweet but dripping—and in my case, dripping and drooping—with infinite wisdom.

When I was a young girl, two men shouted at me while I was walking home from school one day. "Butch!" they had yelled, laughing as they drove away. I remember standing there while my classmates stared, filled with shame and embarrassment. I had no idea at the time I would endure a lifetime of similar incidents. But that scared, intimidated little girl grew up. No matter how many times I was knocked around, with the help of others and my own internal strength, I somehow continued to right myself. Like some giant *Weeble-Wobble.* Apparently, you just can't keep a good butch down. I'm still here. I'm still standing.

ACKNOWLEDGMENTS

For my family and friends who encouraged and supported me constantly over the years. I know it wasn't easy at times. For Amy and your solid friendship and love—you are the definition of integrity. For Christopher Dibble my phenomenal photographer. And for my friends and family who helped make this book a reality. Thank you for your insight and suggestions. You know who you are.